ment Collection

A Handbook
from Victoria L. Young

Management Handbook

Academic Library

Strategic Guide to Information Management

Time Management Handbook for Librarians

J. Wesley Cochran

THE GREENWOOD LIBRARY MANAGEMENT COLLECTION
Gerard B. McCabe, Series Editor

Greenwood Press
NEW YORK • WESTPORT, CONNECTICUT • LONDON

Library of Congress Cataloging-in-Publication Data

Cochran, J. Wesley.
    Time management handbook for librarians / J. Wesley Cochran.
       p.   cm.—(The Greenwood library management collection,
ISSN 0894–2986)
    Includes bibliographical references and index.
    ISBN 0-313-27842-3 (alk. paper)
    1. Librarians—Time management. 2. Library administrators—Time
management. 3. Library employees—Time management. 4. Library
administration. I. Title. II. Series.
Z682. 35. T55C6 1992
025. 1—dc20   91–17120

British Library Cataloguing in Publication Data is available.

Library of Congress Catalog Card Number: 91-17120
ISBN: 0-313-27842-3
ISSN: 0894–2986

First published in 1992

Greenwood Press, 88 Post Road West, Westport, CT 06881
An imprint of Greenwood Publishing Group, Inc.

Printed in the United States of America

∞™

The paper used in this book complies with the
Permanent Paper Standard issued by the National
Information Standards Organization (Z39.48–1984).

10 9 8 7 6 5 4 3 2

Copyright Acknowledgment

The author and publisher gratefully acknowledge permission
to use the following:

Charles Osgood, "The Osgood File." Copyright © 1990 by CBS,
Inc. All rights reserved. Originally broadcast on May 23, 1990
over the CBS Radio Network.

To the memory of Marian Gould Gallagher (1914–1989), whose leadership in librarianship and library education will always be remembered.

Contents

Preface

My introduction to the principles of time management came in 1984 when I was the Associate Law Librarian at the University of Washington. I completed a short staff training course offered to employees, and that experience whetted my appetite for more information on time management, particularly for techniques that librarians could use. I discovered that although business and professional journals frequently publish articles dealing with various aspects of time management, very few journal articles address the concerns of librarians.

By adapting the principles of time management to librarianship, I developed a presentation on the subject for professional library conferences. I discovered that many other librarians, too, were eager to practice effective time management in their careers as well as in their personal lives.

Since libraries operate with two distinct, yet inseparable divisions, they present an interesting environment for the application of time management principles. Technical services operations, for example, possess some of the same characteristics as manufacturing assembly lines. Library resources are acquired, paid for, cataloged, processed, and added to the collection, much like a manufacturer acquires and transforms raw material into a usable product. A library's public services division, too, has corporate counterparts. Librarians seek to inform their clientele of resources available in the collection, like a sales department of a business stimulates interest in a product and a service department helps the customer in using it.

I have organized this book into seven chapters. Chapter 1 deals with time management theories and time management myths. The next three chapters cover techniques for personal work habits and for library staff members. Chapter 5 offers techniques to manage personal and professional time in some special situations. Chapter 6 includes tips for balancing the demands of a career with those in personal life. Finally, chapter 7 describes the steps to follow to put into place a program of effective time management. The appendixes contain forms that one might find helpful in implementing some of the principles of good time management.

Other resources are available on time management to reinforce the principles presented here. Most of the books and articles listed in the annotated bibliography will be readily available locally in academic or public library collections.

I thank the professional librarians and support staff members of the University of Mississippi Law Library and the Texas Tech University Law Library for all of their help and patience during this project, and I particularly honor the memory of Dr. Ellis E. Tucker for his persistence in securing elusive interlibrary loans. I also thank, for their support and encouragement, the members of my family, who know that I, too, need to practice better time management.

1

The Truth about Time Management

"8:47? It can't be that late already!," library director Mary Taylor moaned as she pulled into a parking space. Already Mary was nearly twenty minutes late arriving for work.

The morning routine at Mary's home had not gone well. Ever since her recent divorce, Mary had experienced difficulty getting things done in the morning. Getting her children, Susie, age 6, and Jeff, age 9, ready for school usually proved to be a considerable challenge, and today was no exception.

While Mary was preparing hot cereal for breakfast, Susie announced unexpectedly that she and her two best friends had decided to wear their matching blue polka-dot dresses today, and, of course, Susie's dress was in the dirty clothes bin. Mary explained to Susie that her dress could not be washed and dried in time, and Susie burst into a temper tantrum.

Mary decided to let the tantrum run its course and focused her attention on Jeff.

"Is your homework in your backpack?"

"I did my homework last night, but now I can't find it."

"Have you looked on your desk?"

"Yes, Mom."

"Have you looked in the den?"

"I'll check there now."

"Honestly, Jeff, if you would just put your homework into your backpack when you finished it, we would not have to go through this almost every morning."

Finally, Susie's temper tantrum passed, and she put on the clothes that Mary had picked. Jeff found his homework and put it into his backpack. The family sat down to eat breakfast just in time to be interrupted by a telephone call.

"Mrs. Taylor? This is Laura Smith, Jessica's mother. Since it's Friday, Jessica would like to invite Susie over after school to spend the night." By the time the sleepover was arranged, Mary had to bolt down her breakfast before leaving to take the children to school.

When they arrived at school, Mary realized that she had forgotten to break the $20 bill she had, so she could not give Susie and Jeff money to buy lunch at the cafeteria. Luckily, Bob Johnson, a neighbor from down the street, passed by, walking his son Robby to school.

"Bob, do you have two $1 bills? I don't have the right change for lunch money."

"Sure, no problem. Here you go."

"Thanks, I'll pay you back tonight."

"No hurry."

"That was an almost cruel bit of irony," Mary thought. "I'm always in a hurry."

The commute to the library took longer than usual, so Mary arrived late. After putting things in her office, she went to get coffee. Mary paused and spoke to the staff members congregated around the coffee maker. Although she spent more time around the coffee maker than she thought was perhaps necessary, she felt that visiting with staff members first thing in the morning helped to build morale. After about 20 minutes, she returned to her office.

Mary settled into her chair. Yesterday's mail lay in her in-box. Next to it, the stack of professional journals she was waiting to read had grown. And, it seemed that the unanswered telephone messages had multiplied overnight.

As she sipped her coffee, she tried to remember the solution to a personnel problem that had occurred to her last evening. After struggling to recall, she thought, "I'm sure I will think of it again."

With no particular urgency, Mary then leafed through today's mail that her secretary, Alice, brought in. After handling each item at least once, she put the mail back in her in-box and resolved to take care of the most important things later in the morning. She turned to her calendar and realized that the regional library association meeting was just two weeks away and that she had not begun to work on her presentation that six months ago she promised to deliver. "Time to get started on that," she thought. Turning to her microcomputer, Mary started with the outline. She had barely typed "Introduction" when the phone rang.

"Mary, this is George. The specifications for the library automation RFP are due on Monday, so I thought that we should review it before I send it in."

"I can spare a few minutes if you come to my office now."

Before George arrived, Alice buzzed. "Call for you on line two."

Mary answered the phone to discover a publisher's telemarketing call. Mary ended the call as soon as she thought polite. As she hung up the phone, George, the librarian responsible for the automation project, arrived.

"Come in, George. I have a few minutes before my budget meeting at 10:00."

Mary and George began reviewing the specifications.

"How did you arrive at this figure for the number of workstations that we need? It looks low to me. Didn't you follow the guidelines that the professional staff decided on?"

"Well, I talked to Julie, who drew up the initial plan, and she and I decided . . ."

"What do you mean 'she and I decided'?"

"Mary, sorry to interrupt, but your door was open." Joel, the circulation librarian, stepped in the office and began to describe a problem he perceived concerning the plan for barcoding the collection.

Mary remained seated while Joel took more than a few minutes to outline the problem. "Joel," she finally said, "I am kind of busy right now. Unless the problem relates to the specifications for the automated system, we will have plenty of time later to discuss the problem. So, if you don't mind, I'll think about what you said, and I'll get back to you later."

As Joel turned to leave, Alice buzzed with another phone call. Mary answered quickly. "Mary Taylor . . . Yes, I know what day it is. . . . You know how it is. . . . I'll get right to it. . . . It's next on my agenda, OK? . . . Thanks."

Just after she finished the call, Alice buzzed again, reminding Mary that she was about to be late for her budget meeting with the library department heads.

"George, can we get together again this afternoon? This meeting is likely to last for the rest of the morning."

Mary scooped up her papers for the meeting and hurried off to the library conference room. There she found the library department heads waiting. She started the meeting only to discover that some of the budget figures that she had asked Jane, the acquisitions librarian, to compile were not ready. Jane had not understood that Mary had assigned the task to her.

Rather than end the meeting there, Mary decided that the department heads should discuss the information that was available now. However, several times throughout the meeting, Mary could not answer her department heads' questions because she needed the missing information. After a long, dry discussion, Mary adjourned the meeting.

Following the meeting, Mary glanced at her watch. "11:30? The morning's nearly gone, and already I'm about two hours behind. There has to be a way to get more accomplished."

TIME MANAGEMENT TODAY

Not unlike many librarians, Mary Taylor has more than a few problems managing time in her professional as well as her personal life. By recognizing the challenges facing her and arming herself with some time management strategies, Mary could address the problems that seem to control her time by planning, establishing priorities, limiting interruptions, delegating responsibilities properly, handling telephone solicitations quickly, and conducting meetings properly. Using some standard time management strategies, Mary could ease her frustration at failing to cope well with the pressures of her job and her family.

Too many librarians, like Mary, do not manage their time well because they have never been taught how to do so. Librarians graduate from library school and must abruptly come to grips with supervising support staff members and interacting with other professional librarians, while also trying to find the appropriate balance between career and personal life.

Research into the time management practices of librarians indicates that many share common problems, regardless of the type of library in which they work.[1] While the amount of time spent in specific activities differed somewhat by type of library, the directors of academic, public, state, and special libraries identified meetings, telephone interruptions, drop-in vistors, and attempting too much at once as their most serious time management problems.

In many other professions and businesses, the situation is similar. Few professional schools introduce their graduates to time management theories. So, it should come as no surprise that the subject of time management has never been as popular as it is today. Despite the promise of more leisure time through advances in technology, particularly in the information industry, spare time seems as elusive as ever for most professionals, including librarians.

Recent surveys provide more than ample support for the premise that time appears to be the "most precious commodity in the land."[2] A poll conducted recently by Priority Management Systems, Inc., of executives and business men and women revealed that 85 percent of those surveyed work more than 45 hours per week, 89 percent take work home, 65 percent work more than one weekend each month, 81 percent experience stress (48 percent each day), and 42 percent do not read to their children.[3] And, another recent Harris survey indicated that the average workweek, including commuting, increased from 41 hours in 1973 to 47 hours today and that workweeks for some professions now often exceed 80 hours.[4]

As time at work has increased over the past several decades, the structure of the typical family has changed dramatically. Many households now consist of either two spouses working outside of the home or of a single working parent. As a result, personal time has decreased, even for essential chores such as cooking and shopping. Not surprisingly, in the period from 1970 to 1987, gross retail sales from mail order businesses in the United States rose from $1.8 billion to $3.6 billion (with a high at $4.8 billion in 1984), and gross sales in the restaurant industry rose from $25.5 billion to $135.1 billion.[5]

According to a recent study, women experience a bit more difficulty meeting the demands on their time.[6] Women generally have some 25 percent less leisure time than men, primarily because of the family responsibilities that many women working outside of the home have.

Librarians and other information professionals have experienced the same increasing workloads as other professionals. And, because women comprise a large majority of the library profession, librarians may feel the need for better time management more acutely than other professionals. This need has created heightened interest in better time management.

Further, at the end of the work day, too often it seems that librarians have little to actually show for their efforts. The cataloging backlog may have been reduced temporarily, only to increase when the acquisitions department checks in the latest arrivals, and the requests for reference assistance filled yesterday are replaced by others today.

Without good time management, many people experience low self-esteem and feel that they are not in control of their lives. A sense of being in control is important to high productivity and high self-esteem. Each factor supports the others, and they become a self-fulfilling cycle. One theorist expresses the relationship of the factors as three points on a circle.[7] High productivity promotes a sense of high self-esteem which, in turn, supports a feeling of being in control of events. Being in control of events leads to high productivity, which begins the cycle again.

This desire to be more productive, to feel more in control, and to raise self-esteem has created the demand for seminars, programs, and publications on time management. Several companies now offer day-long seminars on time management and related aspects such as stress reduction and working under pressure. Time management training centers exist in different parts of the country and offer intensive week-long courses in goal-setting and other time management techniques.

Time management "mania" has reached the publishing industry, too. Publishers now offer a variety of titles on the subject, geared to the needs of many professionals, including the clergy, nurses, and attorneys.[8] Professional journals and trade publications also carry a variety of articles on time management from which to choose. Even children have resources available to teach them how to manage time more efficiently.[9]

However, professional library literature provides little for any librarian motivated enough to learn about time management principles on her own. In fact, so little has been written on time management for librarians that the H. W. Wilson index, *Library Literature*, has no subject heading for "Time Management." Instead, it lists what few articles there are with time and motion studies and other related works under the heading "Work Simplification," hardly what most interested librarians would consult first.

Perhaps partly responsible for the lack of resources in librarianship is a perception by some librarians that the concepts of good time management conflict with those of good librarianship. These librarians know that their jobs are based in service to library users, so they equate service to users with availability and generosity. Consequently, they often accept interruptions from library users and fellow staff members, even when they are working on something important, and fail to plan each day in advance, choosing instead to start with the latest request for reference assistance, regardless of pending work that might be more important.

As a result, librarians often experience a sense of not managing time effectively, which may lead to discouragement and problems in motivation. The principles of time management, though, do not contradict the professional principles that librarians espouse. In fact, employing good time management techniques enables librarians to accomplish more, thus allowing them to serve more of the library's clientele while also bringing them closer to realizing their own professional and personal goals.

The techniques of time management that follow provide a framework from which professional librarians in academic, public, and special libraries can benefit. By employing these suggestions, librarians will be able to both formulate a long-term program of time management and address day-to-day time wasters, or what Keith and Howard Schilit call "time leaks."[10]

EXTERNAL FACTORS AFFECTING PERCEPTION OF TIME

To manage time well, one must have a good perception of time, but perception can vary, depending on a number of factors. The time spent while stopped at a red light, for example, may seem quite a bit more than several minutes to a driver in a hurry, but the traffic signals that take the longest to change generally cycle to green in less than two minutes. However, the urgency to drive on makes the cycle seem much longer.

Biological factors play a major role in the way most people deal with time. Some librarians attending a national professional conference, for example, must adjust to a new time zone and battle the fatigue of jet lag for several days. Just as they adjust to the new time zone, the conference ends, and they return home and must re-adjust to their time zone.

Similarly, everyone in the country except those living in a few regions must reset his or her biological clock when daylight saving time begins and ends each year. Immediately after a change, one's perception of the passage of time may be somewhat clouded.

Scientists have theorized that one's biological clock responds to the visual cues of light and darkness received each day. After the sun sets, people sleep. When the sun rises, they awaken. Deprived of these visual cues, one's biological clock would have nothing against which to measure time, and an entirely new pattern of behavior would develop.

In a recent study designed to test the effects of long term isolation for application in deep space exploration, scientists discovered that depriving the subject of the normal visual cues relating to the passage of time affected her biological clock. The subject of the study lived alone without clocks or other time-keeping apparatus for four months in quarters set up in an underground cave. Deprived of the knowledge of the passing of time, the subject changed her "day" over the course of the study. By the end, she tended to sleep for periods between 22 and 24 hours, then awaken and spend up to the next 30 hours in activity.[11]

Emotional stress, too, can affect one's perception of time. For example, the time spent searching for a lost child might seem far longer than it is in reality, and, conversely, the time spent visiting a sick friend or family member in a hospital can seem to pass much faster than it should.

Good time managers take these factors into account and compensate for them when employing the techniques of time management. For example, a good time manager will recognize when she is under stress and become more flexible in what she has planned to accomplish that day.

THE 80/20 PRINCIPLE

Vilfredo Pareto, a nineteenth-century Italian economist and sociologist, developed a theory that significant items in a given group normally constitute a relatively small portion of the total items in the group. Pareto's theory has been popularized as the 80/20 principle.[12]

Studies have shown that the 80/20 principle applies fairly accurately to business. That is, about 80 percent of a firm's business comes from about 20 percent of its customers and, conversely, that about 20 percent of a firm's business comes from about 80 percent of its customers.

Some research indicates that the 80/20 principle applies fairly accurately to some library operations as well. One study found that 28 percent of the serials titles in a medical library accounted for 80 percent of its circulation of serials.[13] So, as a general rule of thumb, the 80/20 principle may be fairly accurate in many library settings.

But, if the 80/20 principle can be applied accurately to a librarian's work patterns as well, some rather depressing results become evident. The 80/20 principle would indicate that 80 percent of the results of librarians' work efforts come from only 20 percent of time spent, meaning that librarians spend 80 percent of their time to get only 20 percent of results. Viewed in that light, it seems apparent that most librarians could benefit from better time management.

MYTHS AND REALITIES OF TIME MANAGEMENT

For some reason, myths about time management abound, both for theory and for practical applications. Librarians, though, may be more receptive to the principles of time management when these myths are exposed, since librarians value decisions based on accurate information.

Most important, good time management does *not* require one to become a slave to a schedule. Some of the worst time managers appear to be organized because they schedule every minute of their work day. But, in fact, they over-schedule, giving themselves too little time to get anything done well in their attempts to get everything done by the end of the day.

Further, using good time management techniques will not cure all personal or library problems. Good time management will not make cataloging backlogs disappear overnight, and following the principles certainly does not mean that one will never be late to work or to an appointment again.

Instead, time management principles provide methods of planning and organizing work, both in the library and at home, to achieve those goals that you consider important. Time management focuses on effectiveness (doing the right job) rather than efficiency (doing a job right).

However, one must expose the accepted myths to understand time management fully.

Myth: Time can be managed.

Reality: People manage themselves and their activities in relation to time. The term *management* denotes control of some type of resource, but time itself cannot be managed. Time continues to pass, minute by minute, hour by hour, regardless of what anyone does. No one can control time because time does not exist in and of itself. Time is the measure of the occurrence of events, but time itself cannot be manipulated. So, time management is not truly the management of time, it is the management of one's activities in relation to time.

Myth: The longer a librarian works (or the harder a librarian works), the more she will accomplish.

Reality: While it may be true that success stems from 1 percent inspiration and 99 percent perspiration, fatigue diminishes all returns. Henry Ford believed that the Model-T automobile would have been into production at least six months earlier than it was if he had limited the amount of overtime worked on the project. Because they were tired, the engineers made errors that took time to diagnose and correct, thus reducing the gains made from the overtime shifts.

Further, regardless of how long one works, a librarian's job performance is judged according to the results that she achieves. So, it makes good sense for librarians to work effectively—to complete their important tasks because those will be the measure of their success.

Myth: If you want something done right, do it yourself.

Reality: It is true that, in some technical areas of library operations, personal creativity might prove disastrous. Not following standard cataloging practices, for example, would create both external and internal problems of consistency and retrievability in the library's catalog. But, if properly done, delegating library work to other staff members can be a valuable time management technique.

Myth: Work cannot be enjoyed.

Reality: Obviously, many, if not most, librarians enjoy their work. Why else would they work for the low pay that they receive, in a profession that suffers from a public relations problem, and for such demanding clients? As a group, librarians are highly motivated people who could be successful in a number of other occupations. Clearly, the enjoyment of the work attracts and holds members of the library profession.

What makes library work frustrating is the sense that one is always behind. Each day's mail and freight deliveries bring more material that must be added to the library's collection, and each day brings more reference questions whether yesterday's questions were answered or not.

Myth: Time management consists of nothing more than traditional time and motion studies to discover how to complete tasks faster.

Reality: While some time and motion studies may be appropriate to diagnose and correct some problems in a library, time management theories focus instead on *effectiveness* (doing the right job), not on efficiency (doing the job right). Concentrating on the right job keeps your attention on the true priorities so that they are handled before they become crises.

Myth: "Time-saving" machines and "time-saving" procedures almost always save time.

Reality: We cannot save time; we can only spend it. Any "savings" in time is actually only a shift in the manner in which we spend time, and time savers may allow us to spend time differently. Often, though, we expect too much from so-called time-saving devices and see very little true difference. We would experience more savings if: (1) the time saver operated as well as its publicity claimed it would, (2) our workloads did not increase correspondingly, and (3) we did not waste what time was saved. But, usually one of the three conditions is not met, effectively cancelling any savings.

Myth: Other people have more time than I do to spend on work, in professional activities, and with family.

Reality: Everyone has the same amount of time each day in which to juggle all personal and professional commitments and priorities. Everyone gets all there is—24 hours—no more and no less. We differentiate ourselves then by how we spend our time. Each one of us decides either by design or neglect what is important and what is not. By focusing on or avoiding certain aspects of our lives, we set our priorities, and these are what occupy the largest share of our time.

Myth: My colleagues seem to get more work done each day than I do.

Reality: Your colleagues might get more done each day than you, but everyone juggles different tasks with different deadlines every day. The belief that some librarians never fall behind and accomplish each day all projects and tasks in the in-box creates in many of us a sense of defeat. The happy truth is that no librarian in any work situation completes every single project every day. Every librarian faces, each day, a variety of priorities and projects that must be juggled. Each day brings new material into the library that must be cataloged, processed, and filed, and every day that a library is open to the clientele brings new demands for service.

Myth: Time management requires following strict rules and a prescribed daily pattern of conduct.

Reality: Time management techniques suggest certain changes in a number of behaviors, particularly in areas such as delegation, interruptions, telephone communications, and planning. But, to be effective, time management must be personal. That is, librarians must adopt and adapt the suggested techniques to fit their own situations. No particular methodology or technique works universally. Further, following a good program of time management should not stifle creativity. Good time managers experiment to find what works best for them.

In fact, some of the most efficient-appearing workers may be so busy being organized that they overlook what a library is all about—serving people. And, to that end, a librarian must work with a variety of other people, both within and without the library. Good time managers do not overlook the development and maintenance of relationships with people.

Myth: We should take pride in working hard.

Reality: Librarians should take pride in working *smart*. Working hard, for its own sake, does little to bolster one's sense of accomplishment. A sense of accomplishment comes instead from handling priority matters efficiently and having time for creative pursuits. Working smarter, not harder, allows librarians to accomplish more in the same amount of time.

RESEARCH IN TIME MANAGEMENT

Recent studies indicate that managers typically spend over one-half of their time in non-managerial activities.[14] Managers spend a considerable portion of each day as technologists, "doing" as opposed to "managing." This comes as no surprise since managers typically come from the ranks of the doers.

The same generally holds true with librarians. Typically, librarians selected for management positions have worked their way up from front-line jobs such as reference and cataloging. So, a typical librarian manager may spend a significant portion of each day in nonmanagerial activities, providing reference service or cataloging.

Although generalization across all types of libraries for all kinds of librarians must be somewhat suspect, most librarians share some characteristics that have implications for indicating appropriate time management techniques. First, as a group, librarians tend to estimate time somewhat unrealistically and accept too many tasks at once. Because librarianship is a service-based profession, librarians pride themselves on their standards of service, attempting to be all things to all people. However, this tendency creates problems for librarians in identifying priorities and limiting interruptions so that the most important work gets done each day.

Second, many librarians feel challenged, and perhaps a bit overwhelmed, by the scope of the information profession today. This comes as a result of several factors, especially the revolution in information technology that has occurred over the past ten years. Just as all revolutions bring changes, the revolution in information technology has brought changes for librarians and other information professionals. Today, librarians must face the challenge of mastering personal computers, CD-ROM products, and a host of other information formats.

Third, a librarian's own professional traits add significant pressure to the sense of lack of accomplishment. As a group, librarians tend to formalize methods and channels of communication. One consequence of formal channels of communication is the number of meetings that librarians plan and attend. Even though the reasons for a regularly scheduled meeting may not be clear, often the participants continue to meet anyway, perhaps partly from habit and partly from a fear that, by not meeting, they might miss something important.

Fourth, in even the smallest of libraries, the work never seems to be completely done. Libraries are dynamic organizations, so each day brings new books to be added to the collection and new reference questions to answer. Rarely being able to celebrate closure of one project before moving to the next, many librarians feel that they spend most of their days running to keep up, rather than running to stay ahead.

Although specific responsibilities of staff members vary considerably from library to library, research indicates that librarians share many characteristics in their positions and, consequently, many time management problems. A British survey indicated that planned meetings occupy the largest share (33.7 percent) of library managers' time. Planned meetings were followed by general paperwork (17.9 percent), unplanned meetings (15.0 percent), writing reports (8.8 percent), reading reports

(4.6 percent), and reading mail (4.6 percent). Other common activities included writing letters and memos, reading journals, handling mail, and placing and answering telephone calls.[15]

Library directors also share many time management problems. A recent survey revealed that library directors reported committee work, problems in delegation, taking on too much work at the same time, and failing to identify goals and priorities as major time management problems.[16]

In addition, academic library and public library directors must also deal with clientele who feel entitled to participate in the library decision-making process. Faculty members and students besiege academic library directors, and members of the general public seek avenues of participation in decisions affecting public libraries. The participation process creates challenges for the effective time manager.

Library directors also identify many of the same challenges and time pressures as problems of time management that other professionals do. Thus, librarians can use many of the same techniques that executives and other professionals use for managing time effectively.

In formulating a plan for time management, each librarian must realize that techniques that work well in one particular library may not work well in another, due in part to variations from institution to institution. While one might assume that librarians follow a more or less universal job description, recent studies indicate otherwise.[17] In reality, librarians' duties differ greatly from employer to employer. Just as school libraries differ from special libraries and academic libraries differ from public libraries, so, too, do the responsibilities of the librarians working there. As a result, no time management theory or strategy will be universally applicable, and each librarian must evaluate the strategies presented here in light of the practical realities of specific libraries.

Further, just as librarians differ in their professional aspirations as well as working styles, so, too, can managers. The larger the library, the more room there is for different management styles among managers. The best results occur, of course, when the style of the library manager matches that of the staff. However, managers must be flexible enough to vary their styles when their preferred style does not work well in a particular setting.

APPROACHES TO TIME MANAGEMENT

Two basic time management theories dominate the literature today. Most resources are based in one or both of these theories, and, in fact, both theories complement each other. Neither theory is complete without some of the structural underpinnings of the other.

As a result, most resources rely heavily on the major points from both theories, varying only in the level of detail of coverage provided. Most of the works included in the bibliography of this book are based on these major theories, and the main themes appear in many works on time management.

In most settings, librarians deal with four types of time demands at work: supervisor time, organizational time, coworker time, and personal work time.[18] The demands that supervisors and coworkers place on one's work time are easily recognized, as well as the category of personal work time. The routines required by the library's institution or community, such as annual reports, that place demands on a librarian's time comprise the organizational category.

At first impression, it might appear that librarians have little control over the time demands from supervisors, institutions, and coworkers. However, time management techniques can be used in all of these areas as well as for a librarian's personal time.

Traditional Theory

Many of the resources in time management produced in the last fifteen years restate and advance the work done by Alan Lakein.[19] Lakein focuses on goalsetting through the use of three questions: What are my lifetime goals? How would I like to spend the next three years? and, If I knew I would be struck dead by lightning six months from today, how would I live until then? Lakein also advocates the use of specific behaviors and techniques to eliminate time wasters.

Values-Based Theory

Charles Hobbs developed a method of time management in *Time Power* that supports establishing goals based on one's values.[20] According to Hobbs, the frustration and the sense of not accomplishing much stems from the dissonance that results between that which is valued both professionally and personally and the actual activities of a work day. Too often, we see little relation between the things that occupy our time each day and what we value as important.

Hobbs believes that typical work activities do not relate directly to personal and professional goals, or one's own sense of goals, if they have not been articulated clearly, and this lack of relation creates dissonance or anxiety. One fails to accomplish what is important because time is spent in activities that seemingly lead nowhere.

Hobbs's theory involves first recognizing personal values, called unifying principles, for both personal and professional life. Next, one establishes goals and objectives in harmony with these unifying principles. Finally, one develops strategies to achieve the objectives and attain the goals that have been established.

In identifying one's unifying principles, one first must recognize the attributes and principles that are important personally. For example, one might identify "Have a close and supportive family life" as one of the unifying principles.

Then, under the system, one establishes goals in harmony with those principles. To support the "family life" principle, for instance, one could list "Spend more time with family members" as a goal. Then, to establish objectives designed to help attain the goal, one could list specific activities such as "Attend 75 percent of baseball games," "Play with the children after work at least three times per week," and "Plan one special activity for each weekend."

Hobbs's theory can be illustrated by two circles, the first representing the unifying principles and the established goals and objectives and the second circle the activities in the action plan. To the extent that the circles intersect, the less dissonance one will experience. When one's activities do not relate directly to the goals and objectives established in support of one's unifying principles (i.e., the circles do not intersect), one experiences dissonance, the frustration that one's efforts and accomplishments seemingly do not mean much. Changing one's activities to support personal values (i.e., bringing the circles to a significant intersection), lessens the dissonance.

Having these specific goals and activities identified lessens the dissonance that one might feel leaving in the middle of a meeting or putting down a project before it is complete to attend a child's baseball game or scouting activity. Seeing how these actions support one of the guiding principles results in less frustration and anxiety.

Motivation

Motivation also plays a large part in the success of any time management plan. Even though most of the techniques are easy to learn and to implement, everyone at some time has one of "those" days, when the simplest plans fall apart. Then, even the best time managers must fight the library "forest fires" and quiet the crises as best they can.

In 1954, Abraham Maslow, one of the early motivational theorists, published his philosophy of the Hierarchy of Human Needs.[21] That hierarchy is often illustrated as a pyramid. Maslow theorized that each person has a set of hierarchical needs: survival, safety, belonging, and esteem. As a person satisfied the needs in a lower level, he moved to the next higher level.

But, in response to external developments, that person could also regress to a lower level on the pyramid. For example, the lowest level of the pyramid, survival, consists of the basic needs of food, clothing, and shelter. Regardless of how high up we are on the pyramid, if a tree falls on our house, for that day, and probably for several more after that, we will regress to that first level of the pyramid—basic needs. Instead of attending to a need at a higher level, we will give almost undivided attention to satisfying the need of providing shelter.

Motivation affects time management in much the same way. No matter how effective or motivated a librarian may be in managing time, there will be some day when a personal or work-related crisis will force a reaction, rather than an action from the established plan. In such a situation, it is likely that the reactionary behavior will serve to undermine what would normally be considered effective time management.

However, once the crisis has passed, anyone can start again by employing the techniques presented here. Techniques of time management are remarkably versatile, so most librarians will be able to adapt them generally for both professional and personal use.

Some librarians may find that they already use some of the techniques presented here as strategies for good time management, and other techniques may appear to be obvious. But, librarians are challenged so often that they tend to become accustomed to expecting the difficult. As a result, sometimes they may overlook the obvious.

One recent study has indicated that time management techniques are fairly easy to learn and implement.[22] That study also found that the most effective method of implementing the techniques included both training and practice. Thus, the techniques presented here will be most effective when library staff members approach time management as a group project, as discussed later, and give and receive feedback to each other on the effectiveness of implementation.

The following chapters include tips for dealing with the challenges for effective time management presented at work and home by coworkers and family members. And, the last chapter discusses preparations for implementing a program for time management.

2

Personal Time Management Techniques

Effective time managers use a variety of techniques in their personal work patterns so that they accomplish more of their important tasks each day. This chapter focuses on these techniques, while the next chapter covers techniques to improve time management in work patterns involving coworkers and supervisors.

Librarians, like other professionals, experience frustration when they spend seemingly endless hours in work without achieving anything of real value. And, librarians can become frustrated with normal library operations. For example, most libraries always have a cataloging backlog. While at certain times during the year the backlog may be smaller than at other times, the backlog rarely goes away completely because each new day brings new books, videotapes, records, and other items to be added to the library's collection. In other words, the task of cataloging in most libraries is never finished because the collection is always growing.

Much in the same way, the reference departments of many libraries struggle to keep up with the demand for information. The librarians there must continually judge the incoming reference requests to handle those that are truly urgent as quickly and as accurately as possible, while still not postponing too long those earlier, less urgent requests.

In these situations, then, many librarians feel the frustration of never completely finishing a task or of not keeping up with demand. While this type of frustration might indicate a time management difficulty in other organizations, the unique nature of library operations lies at the heart of the problem. To some degree, the frustration that librarians may experience about not finishing a task may be a matter of perception.

Too often, it seems that librarians focus on tasks that they have not accomplished—books remaining to be cataloged, reference questions to be answered, and looseleaf service releases to be filed—rather than on those that they have completed. In fact, a librarian may have accomplished many important tasks, but she may obscure her achievements because she emphasizes the negative—those tasks left undone—instead of accentuating the positive.

This sense of frustration can interfere and obscure what is truly important in one's personal life, too. If a librarian takes an hour off, for example, to see her son in his school play, she might feel some guilt in leaving work to be done behind, and she might be tempted to characterize the situation as a problem of time management. But, effective time management supports the achievement of both personal and professional goals. So, by recognizing her true values, one of which might be to develop a healthy, supportive family, she could acknowledge that attending a child's play helps to achieve a personal goal, thereby lessening the sense of guilt at leaving work to be done.

THE IMPORTANCE OF PLANNING

Thoreau expressed the value of planning when he said, "In the long run, men hit only what they aim at."[1] And, the antithesis of Thoreau's statement is also true. If a person aims at nothing, he will probably hit it. Only from a set of well-defined goals can one develop a set of strategies for action as well as evaluation criteria for measuring success.

Librarians, as a group, appreciate the value of planning. Good library operation involves a large amount of long-range, mid-range, and short-term planning, so librarians at all levels understand how important planning is. For example, most library managers know fairly accurately when their physical plants will exhaust growth space. They know that new buildings or additions must be planned far in advance, so they monitor the available growth space very closely. Similarly, librarians concerned with budget planning usually know very well how much of the library's budget each year is encumbered for serial costs and how much is available for new book purchases. The budget plans must be accurate to avoid fiscal problems.

The reason for this sophistication in planning is self-evident. If a library fails to plan for growth or for budgeting, the consequences are likely to be disastrous. Governing bodies typically do not appreciate learning of library space or budget problems after they have reached crisis levels. Instead, the politic librarian will raise these issues early in a long-term planning process.

Since librarians appreciate the value of planning, one would assume that they incorporate planning into their personal work habits. And, while perhaps some do, many do not. After all, like the curricula of other professional schools, the typical library school curriculum focuses on more substantive matters and generally ignores teaching practical skills.

SETTING GOALS AND OBJECTIVES

The first step in any effective time management program involves identifying personal and professional values and establishing goals and objectives in support of those values, as described in the previous chapter. All else in effective time management stems from this process. Chapter 7, "Implementing a Time Management Plan," also contains information to assist librarians interested in beginning a program of effective time management, and the appendixes contain forms that may be helpful in establishing goals and objectives.

Goal setting begins with an understanding of how values affect the planning process.[2] Even at a sub-conscious level, personal values influence everyone, so it is appropriate to take personal values into account during the planning process.

If you have trouble stating personal values, consult some of the books and other sources listed in the bibliography that provide particular guidance in this area. Often, these resources provide sets of forms that will help; consult the forms contained in the appendixes as well.

Daniel Stamp identifies the six "yous" that one should consider to determine true personal values: workplace you, involved with career and retirement; intellectual you, concerned with self-development; physical you, requiring exercise and proper diet; family you, involved with special activities with spouse and children; social you, concerned with pressures and opportunities from friends; and spiritual you, concerned with religious and meditative aspects.[3] One must consider matters related to each of these aspects of his life to determine personal values.

Charles Hobbs uses values, what he calls unifying principles,[4] as the beginning point for his system of time management. A person using Hobbs's approach starts by identifying those principles either that affect him the most or that he wants to guide his life.

For example, a librarian may decide that her life is guided by many principles, including, for example, these three: striving for excellence in the library profession, having personal integrity, and creating and maintaining a close and supportive family life. Under Hobbs's theory, people must decide the correct number of principles for themselves. There is no magic number, but people listing only one principle have probably not listed all of the principles that guide their lives. Likewise, those who list fifty or more have probably either duplicated other principles on the list or have moved from the level of unifying principles to the level of goals and objectives.

After listing the unifying principles guiding your life, move to the next level, and identify long-term goals that support your unifying principles. Include goals related to your profession and to your personal life.

Using one of the examples above, if one of your unifying principles relates to having a close and supportive family, you might identify long-term goals like "Develop closer relationships with spouse and children," and "Be actively involved in the children's education."

After identifying the goals that support a particular unifying principle, establish objectives that, when satisfied, will help you attain the goals that you have set. To reach the goal of developing closer relationships with your spouse and children, you might formulate the objectives, "Provide a significant alternate learning experience for the family each month," "Volunteer in a leadership role for one of the children's extracurricular activities," and "Spend one evening out each month with my spouse."

Then, create an action plan to satisfy these objectives. To become involved in your children's extracurricular activities, volunteer as a scout leader or baseball coach or undertake an extracurricular activity of the children's and your own design. For example, you might spend time with your children building and running a lemonade stand to teach values related to goal setting and financial management.

Having these goals and objectives established is crucial to the success of a time management program because all other techniques should be based on attaining the identified goals. Without goals and objectives in place, employing the following techniques would not be true time management because one would not experience an increase in the amount of work accomplished. Time management is not just avoiding situations that waste one's time; it also involves techniques to accomplish more of what is important. Because goals and objectives are essential to focus one's work efforts, the first step in any time management program is establishing them.

THE DAILY PLAN

Starting from the goals and objectives established, a good time manager develops a plan of action each day. This daily plan will determine whether one achieves his objectives and attains his goals since it provides direction for one's work efforts. Activities listed on a daily plan that do not directly support the goals and objectives that one has identified serve only to distract one from the true priority tasks.

Further, as circumstances change from day to day, so must one's priorities. Librarians work in an environment that is constantly changing, so they must revise their plans accordingly. Each day brings new books and other items to add to the collection, new reports to prepare, and new reference questions to answer. One of the keys to time management is to focus each day's efforts on the activities that are truly important in realizing one's established goals.

Successful time managers plan each day by preparing a list of priority tasks and a work and appointment schedule. That is, they formulate a plan for each day rather than simply react to what the day brings. By doing so, they continue to focus on what is important in reaching their goals.

Creating the list of priority tasks for the day starts as simply as writing a list of things to do. However, a true list of priority tasks involves much more. A typical list of things to do does not identify the tasks by priority. By proceeding down the list, completing each task in order, one might leave some very important task unfinished simply because it was not at the top of the list.

When the list of things to do for the day is complete, identify the high, medium, and low priorities by relating each task to objectives and goals previously identified. If the task directly supports the achievement of an important goal, assign it a high priority. Assign a low priority to those tasks which do not support the achievement of goals, and rank the remaining tasks—those that indirectly support goals and objectives—somewhere between the high and low priorities.

Alan Lakein suggests using the letters A-B-C to denote high-, medium- and low-priority rankings;[5] other writers suggest other notations, including Ace-King-Jack-Deuce.[6] Regardless of the ranking nomenclature used, the purpose remains the same: to identify the priority tasks that focus energies on achieving goals that are truly important.

Richard Winwood expresses the relationship of the list of priority tasks to goals as a pyramid with four levels.[7] A person's governing values, what Hobbs calls unifying principles, form the base of the pyramid. The long-range goals and intermediate goals form the next levels, respectively. And, the list of priority tasks, what Winwood calls the daily task list, tops the pyramid.

Viewing the daily planning process in that manner, one can see clearly that the most important daily tasks must be based on goals and objectives that have been identified and developed. Personal and work activities that bear no relationship to these goals or objectives create significant time management problems. They create stumbling blocks to achieving the most important tasks and create a sense at the end of a day that nothing important has been accomplished.

One might think that, because librarians generally appreciate the value of planning, they also realize the need for establishing priorities among those tasks on the daily list. But, librarians may, in fact, have particular difficulty setting certain priorities for philosophical reasons.

Contemporary professional philosophy encourages equality of service and discourages placing a higher value on one person's information needs than another's; in certain libraries, policies based on this philosophy might work well. But this approach ignores the realities in which most libraries must operate. One reality is that all library users are not created equal.[8] Academic librarians, for example, chiefly serve the members of the academic institution. Services for the general public come after them. And, special librarians tend to serve only the employees of their institutions. So, despite the egalitarian ideals of the profession, most libraries have some sort of pecking order that each librarian must consider when identifying the priority tasks each day.

Librarians also avoid placing a higher value on one aspect of library operations than another. Obviously, good public services depend heavily on good technical services, and vice versa. But, assigning higher priority to tasks that involve direct service to library users promotes good public relations. Giving reference assistance to a library user waiting at the reference desk, for example, should rank higher in priority than filing cards in the catalog. However, since good reference service depends to a large degree on a catalog that is current, the filing cannot be overlooked continually. Nevertheless, when faced with an immediate need to prioritize, one should lean toward the task that delivers library service to the library user.

The basic nature of the technical services operations in most libraries also creates some difficulty for librarians trying to establish priorities. The acquisitions, cataloging, and processing operations comprise an assembly line of sorts as titles are added to the library's collection. Assigning a low priority to some part of the process will slow it down, cause backlogs, and idle some library workers. So, one must take that reality into account when establishing priorities so that important routines will not be neglected.

A technique called a *preview review* can help identify the real priority tasks for the day.[9] At the start of each day, a librarian should think ahead to the end of the day when she will have a sense of satisfaction and accomplishment from having completed the most important tasks for the day. Then, she should identify the tasks that would provide that sense of accomplishment and designate those as the high priorities for the day.

Obviously, a library is a dynamic environment. And, in such an environment, daily priorities can change. As such, one should identify the priority tasks anew each day. Evaluate the tasks left undone in light of each day's needs and demands. In that way, you will continue to focus on the truly important tasks for the day.

In assigning priorities, do not automatically assign a high priority to urgent tasks. Distinguish between those tasks that are truly important and those that seem urgent, but are not important. Important tasks are those that directly support the attainment of your goals. Urgent tasks are those that call for your attention. Some important tasks may also be urgent, but all urgent tasks are not important.

For example, if a person chooses to answer the telephone while working on something important, she has bowed to the pressure of the urgent. The telephone call proclaims its urgency, sometimes quite loudly. However, the telephone call's urgency is no guarantee of importance. Unfortunately, a librarian conditioned to respond to requests might react first to the urgent, without considering the relative importance of the task. Allowing the interruption diverts one's attention from what she has recognized as important.

Be flexible so that you can respond to external circumstances. Flexibility is a key to effective time management. Even though you might begin the day with proper planning and a list of priority tasks, if the library director calls with a project that must be completed quickly, you must respond to that circumstance. When those occasions arise, you have to re-prioritize the list of tasks in the daily plan and work from there.

Keep the list of each day's priority tasks in sight as a constant reminder to focus efforts on what is important. One library student worker learned the value of keeping his list in plain sight. Each day, he wrote his list on the back of his hand.

Every library employee has a different view of what is important to accomplish each day. As such, library supervisors should review with their staff members their lists of priority tasks each day. Without direct communication with them concerning the daily priorities, the staff members will not know how they can best support the library.

A daily review of priorities with library staff members also allows them to have input in establishing priorities and gives supervisors the opportunity to make adjustments if the staff members' lists differ substantially from their own list. Obviously, the more that a supervisor can support the completion of staff members' priority tasks and staff can support the completion of a supervisor's priority tasks, the closer both staff and supervisor will be to attaining the goals that they have established.

Supervisors must consider the current workloads of staff members when coordinating assignments of priority tasks. If a library staff member already has three major projects, for example, her supervisor cannot realistically expect that staff member to take on another one and maintain the same level of quality.

Just as important as discussing priorities with staff members is discussing priorities with supervisors on a regular basis. The frequency of these discussions, obviously, will depend on one's position. A reference librarian, for example, may have daily discussions with his supervisor, while a public library director may have monthly discussions with the city manager. The form of these discussions can vary, too, depending on the desires of those involved. Brief, informal meetings may be appropriate for some librarians and supervisors, while others might prefer more formal meetings.

WORK AND APPOINTMENT SCHEDULE

Besides priority tasks, an effective daily plan also depends on a second component, a work and appointment schedule. Obviously, you will have commitments to other people. Planned and unplanned meetings take the largest share of a librarian's typical day, and telephone communications will take another large part.

But, the work and appointment schedule goes beyond a traditional appointment calendar. In addition to reserving time for others in meetings and other commitments, an effective work and appointment schedule will include time reserved for commitments to yourself. A good time manager schedules the work she wants to accomplish each day as a commitment to herself. Work time reserved for yourself comprises an important part of your daily schedule.

Much of a librarian's work day consists of recurring tasks, work normally done every day, such as cataloging books or answering reference questions. In establishing the daily work and appointment schedule, a librarian should know about how much of the day should be devoted to these recurring tasks. For example, a librarian whose duties include cataloging should know approximately how much time to devote to it each day in order to keep books moving through the acquisitions process.

Knowledge of the time usually required for these recurring tasks is essential for a librarian to formulate a realistic daily work and appointment schedule. A common problem among directors in all types of libraries is underestimating the amount of time required for particular tasks.[10] To allow for unexpected interruptions, add 20 percent to the time estimate for recurring tasks.

Quiet Time

In building each day's schedule, librarians should not overlook the fact, though, that they owe themselves the same courtesy given others—their time and undivided attention. Make a commitment to getting your own work done by scheduling some time each day to concentrate on those tasks that you have identified as high priority. For example, several days before the deadline for a big report to the library director, a librarian should set aside some time so that it will be finished on schedule. Then, on the day that the report is due, time should be reserved so that last minute adjustments can be made and preliminary results can be discussed with the library director. All of these commitments should be reflected in the work and appointment schedules for those days.

In fact, all librarians need some time each day for quiet, concentrated work, scheduled like any other appointment. Reserving quiet time each day fulfills a librarian's commitment to herself. The daily work routine for most professional librarians is full of interruptions. To be able to devote the time necessary to important reports, projects, and other tasks, every librarian must have some time scheduled each day for concentrated work.

Limit outside interruptions during your quiet time each day so that you can use the opportunity to focus on and complete your high priority tasks. Some time management theorists recommend not allowing any interruptions during this time, but that approach is unrealistic for most librarians. Few can afford the luxury of *complete* solitude. No academic library director, for example, could afford to be unavailable to the university president for long periods of time, just as no special library director could be unavailable to corporate officials and no public library director could be unavailable to the mayor or city manager.

If you have difficulty scheduling time for yourself to concentrate on priority tasks because of scheduled commitments to others, try to designate one day each week as a "quiet" day. For that day, limit appointments with others as much as possible and avoid planned and unplanned meetings. Further, have the library secretary or receptionist limit telephone interruptions to provide you with more time for concentrated work.

In scheduling quiet time for concentrated work, take into account the factor of your biological clock. Most people know the time of day that they are at their best, so schedule your best time of day as quiet time. Use those hours to concentrate on the tough, priority tasks. Attack those tasks then, and resist the temptation to use that time for less important, though perhaps more appealing, matters such as reading mail or handling routine matters.

Most people function best during the first hours of the morning. At midmorning, energy levels then tend to drop. Following lunch, most people experience an increase in energy until midafternoon. Even knowing that, most people work ineffectively because they lose their most productive hours of the day. When they first arrive at work, rather than beginning to focus on the priority tasks immediately, they spend time getting coffee, chatting with other staff members about matters not related to work, and the like. They spend time in the "opening ceremonies" of the day, rather than using their most productive time for work.

Visiting with coworkers is not unimportant. Most library staff members, particularly those in support staff positions, work hard at jobs that can best be described as sometimes tedious and exacting, but always important. Many are true unsung heroes since the good work that they do goes largely unnoticed by most library clientele, but their errors seem to come to everyone's attention. So, building and maintaining morale among library staff members is very important. But, if you are at your best first thing in the morning, focus first on work, and save visiting with staff members for your morning break.

Combine Work Routines

When setting up the work schedule each day, look for opportunities to combine routines. For example, librarians who are responsible for collection development usually receive dozens of promotional flyers sent by book publishers by bulk-rate postage each week, and many of these flyers are duplicate copies of those sent to the library earlier. Librarians can use this as an opportunity to combine routines and thereby be more effective at managing time. Rather than handle each of these flyers every day, a collection development librarian would be more effective having a secretary or clerk first sort the flyers once each week to eliminate duplicates. Then, rather than dealing with incoming flyers every day, the librarian will handle them just once each week, without the bother of duplicate mailings.

In preparing each daily schedule, look for similar opportunities to batch tasks. Obviously, one must take care in batching tasks because it involves a conscious decision to delay, albeit for better efficiency later. Since librarians often function under tremendous time pressures dictated by the library's clientele, the needs of the client must be considered paramount and may require alteration of carefully made plans.

However, in some situations, one can batch routines to eliminate duplicate effort. With common routines such as catalog searches and book processing, librarians often spend about the same time preparing for several items as for one. So, to save time overall, unless, for example, there is some special reason to process a single book—such as one requested immediately by the library's primary clientele—usually one can wait until there are several to do.

Use Tickler Systems

Another important technique related to the work and appointment schedule is to develop a tickler system for recurring events that will help you with advance planning. Using a tickler will save any librarian a good deal of aggravation. Tasks no longer have to be last minute because they have been overlooked.

For example, most academic libraries circulate holiday operating schedules to their faculties early in December each year, so an appropriate note in the library director's tickler file for November would be to prompt the appropriate librarian or staff member responsible for publicizing the schedule to put it together. By prompting the action well in advance, the tickler will help avoid last-minute time pressures.

WHEN TO MAKE THE DAILY PLAN

When to plan each day's schedule is largely a personal choice. Some librarians take time at the beginning of each day for planning, while others choose the late afternoon for planning the next day. Of course, the most important aspect of planning is to establish a work plan each day, but most people find that taking 10 to 15 minutes at the end of the day to plan for the following day has several benefits over making the day's plan in the morning.

First, planning in the afternoon helps bring each day's events to a close, so you will much be less likely to bring the concerns of work home with you. As such, you can give more attention to family as well as personal concerns.

Second, interruptions tend to come less frequently at the end of the day than at the beginning, so you will be more likely to complete your list of priorities and work and appointment schedule in a less stressful situation. This will permit time to make thoughtful, reasoned decisions about the priorities for the next day, rather than hurrying to get planning done so that you can handle the first major crisis of the day.

Third, planning at the end of the day rather than at the beginning also provides the opportunity to review the accomplishments of the day. If one waits until the morning to plan, the chances increase that the priority tasks that await will loom so large that they will overshadow, if not totally obscure, successes from the day before. Good time managers seek to accentuate the positive, and thus their accomplishments, whenever possible.

Finally, and most important, planning for the following day in the afternoon puts into place a plan that allows you to hit the ground running each morning. So, you can take advantage of the morning hours for high-quality productivity. One can devote time to getting things done, rather than planning to make them happen.

Regardless of when you choose to make it, you should begin each work day with a plan. Failing to plan is, in reality, planning to fail. Failing to plan is like going to the grocery store without a shopping list. You are likely to buy some important items, but forget others. Planning helps get the right things done, those tasks that you have identified as important because they relate to the goals that you want to achieve. Instead of reacting to situations, you anticipate problem areas before they become crises and thus assume a measure of control over your work. You control it; it does not control you.

Using a Commercial Calendar System

Some people choose one of several printed commercial calendar systems to help them plan and prioritize each day's tasks. A typical system goes far beyond providing an appointment calendar. Usually such a system includes space for listing the daily priority tasks in a location that tends to keep them in sight, so that those priority tasks are not forgotten. Popular systems include Day-Timers[11] and Quo Vadis.[12]

Using a Microcomputer to Plan

If you use a microcomputer daily, consider one of a number of *personal information manager* programs that support management of priorities. Generally, a good program will provide not only the ability to store your appointment calendar but also your list of tasks to do with priority rankings.

Many of the most popular programs also provide a small free-text database feature that permits the user to add notes about any task or meeting. The program, in effect, becomes an electronic file cabinet, storing the notes until the user needs them. Since librarians tend to juggle many projects or requests on an ongoing basis, this feature may be among the most valuable. Among the most popular programs are: Arriba,[13] Current,[14] Instant Recall,[15] OnTime,[16] PackRat,[17] Primetime Personal,[18] SideKick,[19] and who–what–when.[20]

FOCUS ON THE PRIORITIES

Start each day's plan work plan with time allocated for the high-priority tasks, and focus on those tasks during your periods of high energy. Continue to work on the high-priority tasks until you have either completed them or reached a point where more information is needed or assistance is required. With major library projects, often librarians must coordinate information coming from several different sources, and the flow of information from all sources may not come together at the same time. When you reach a dead end on one task, do what you can to solve the problem, then move on to the next task.

Further, to keep on track throughout the work day, you should follow Alan Lakein's advice and ask yourself frequently: what is the best use of my time *right now*?[21] Asking the question after finishing a phone call or after a staff member's interruption forces you to back to your list of priority tasks and to what you consider important to accomplish.

Another important point to remember in keeping focused on the high-priority tasks is to resist the temptation of distractions. The mail that a library receives is one of the greatest distractions for librarians. However, you should resist the temptation to deal with mail until the end of your quiet work period. With very few exceptions—interlibrary loans often being one of those—mail can wait. Little that comes in the mail carries the potential to require reorganizing a carefully established list of priorities. However, far too often, librarians spend some of their most productive time reading correspondence when higher priority tasks await.

Further, although they know that they should begin each day by working on high-priority tasks, too often most people choose to start with lower-ranked tasks during peak times. Low-priority tasks generally are smaller and less complicated, which is why they are usually less important, and they can be completed in a relatively short period of time. So, most people focus on them first and take great delight in scratching them off of their lists of priority tasks. But, whatever sense of accomplishment found in completing lower-ranked priorities above those that are ranked highest is illusory. At the end of the day, those highest-ranked priorities will remain undone, the real effect being that little progress has been made toward attaining one's goals.

Some successful business executives in top corporations focus on their high-priority items by arriving regularly one hour or more before their offices normally open. They use those hours as their quiet time for concentrated work. Even as an occasional strategy, this technique can work well for librarians to provide a running start to the day. However, for librarians balancing the demands of their careers with those of their families, this option may not always be available.

Another strategy for remaining with high-priority tasks until they are completed is to reward yourself for completing a hard or unpleasant task. The reward can be anything that you enjoy: watching an old movie, reading the latest novel, or going to a baseball game. By providing an additional incentive, you may work just a bit harder to complete those most important tasks.

TIME WINDFALLS

Time "windfalls" are unexpected periods of idle time that present themselves throughout the day. These small periods of time can be windfalls to your work and appointment schedule if you prepare correctly to exploit them. For example, a librarian who takes the latest issue of a professional journal along with her for an appointment is prepared to take advantage of a time windfall that might occur if she is asked to wait at the other person's office. She can put that waiting time to her use, rather than sitting idle.

Several strategies can help you to be prepared for time windfalls. First, take work with you when you visit another's office so that you can use as work time what you would normally spend waiting. Second, keep a windfall file by your desk and take it with you when you travel or just go down the hall to meet someone else so that you can take advantage of the time. Your windfall file should contain nonurgent tasks such as journal articles and other correspondence that you have been intending to read that you can now review quickly before the next appointment begins.

If your library operates with a dictation system that uses cassettes or microcassettes, investigate the possibility of getting a portable dictation unit if you do not already have one. Having a portable dictation unit available allows you to convert what would otherwise be "down" time into work time, wherever you happen to be. You need not use the system only for letters and memos. You can dictate adjustments to your calendar, notes made while traveling, and other information that you need.

PROCRASTINATION

An old English proverb, "One of these days is none of these days," too often rings true. Business executives routinely identify procrastination as one of the major problems facing business today.

Causes of Procrastination

1. Fear of Failure

Fear of failure is one reason for procrastinating, so some may delay making hard decisions in an effort to prevent failing. Librarians facing tough decisions should analyze their situations to put the decision into perspective.

First, how much will the decision matter six months from now? If the matter has few or no long term consequences, and many decisions will fit this category, you will usually be able to correct any mistake made now. So, you should not worry to the point of feeling stressed about making a decision and thus procrastinate.

Second, what is the worst that could happen to you as result of an incorrect decision? Obviously, you could lose your job, but that seldom happens on the basis of just one mistake. And even if it does, many librarians have sought and found jobs on short notice, so the real effect of a bad decision is likely to be minimal.

2. Fear of Success

As contradictory as it seems, some people fear succeeding, particularly with complex tasks or tasks that they find unpleasant. If they handle those well (i.e., they succeed), they suspect that more of this kind of work will come their way. And, this may be in libraries generally. Because libraries often have less flexibility in providing rewards, monetary or other, than many organizations, the reward for good work may indeed be more work.

At the same time, these people may not want to fail, so this creates a no-win dilemma that increases anxiety and encourages procrastination. They secretly hope that the task will disappear, relieving their anxiety.

3. Avoiding Judgment

Some people procrastinate because they want to avoid making judgments in difficult situations. By postponing a decision, they believe that the problem may solve itself. However, no serious problem just goes away, so the delay in diagnosis simply means a delay in achieving a solution.

4. Feeling of Hopelessness

Librarians in particular can fall victim to a certain sense of hopelessness because of the never-ending nature of work in a library. Why struggle to keep up since every day brings more work to be done?

5. Lack of Urgency

Some people may be tempted to postpone tasks that have no sense of urgency about them. They believe the myth that they work better under pressure. In fact, most people create more errors when under pressure, and the stress that working under pressure creates causes even more time management problems.

6. Avoiding Unpleasant Work

Many people dislike some aspects of their jobs, and library staff members typically are no different. Some of the work in the operation of a library is not particularly interesting or stimulating, but it has to be done for the library to operate smoothly. Staff members who attempt to avoid unpleasant or boring tasks by postponing them can create significant problems and impair the library's mission of prompt delivery of information services.

7. Feeling Overwhelmed

One recent study indicates that the more complex a task is, the more anxiety it creates.[22] Some workers may experience difficulty getting started on large projects simply because of the size and scope of the endeavor. Projects such as library automation involve countless hours of planning and work, so staff members beginning the process may feel somewhat intimidated at the undertaking.

8. Personal Control

People who procrastinate, in fact, exercise a measure of control, however small, over a particular matter. By holding up progress on some project, they can show that they have power to manipulate the process, and, for some library staff members, exercising even a small amount of control over their workload proves their importance to the library.

9. The Procrastination Habit

Some people procrastinate simply because they have incorporated the practice into their work routine. Procrastination can be habit-forming, and, thus, it can become the established routine at work.

10. Lack of Information

Occasionally, one might need to collect some information to be able to handle a particular matter. And, delaying a decision for needed information may be the only appropriate reason for procrastination, but only if one takes steps to collect the information in a prompt manner. Otherwise, the reason loses its credibility.

Strategies for Fighting Procrastination

1. Set strict personal rules against bringing work home, working on weekends, and working late.

Bringing work home has been a standard practice for many executives over the years, and the availability of laptop computers today makes it even easier to do. But if you permit yourself to think, I can stay late, or, I will finish this at home, or, I will work over the weekend, you will tend to accomplish less at the library during regular hours. Instead of focusing your efforts on the priority tasks of the day, you tempt yourself to postpone working. However, if you set strict rules against bringing work home, working on weekends, and working late, at the very least, your family members will benefit, and you will have newly found time for hobbies, church activities, and civic groups.

2. *Make a realistic appraisal of the situation.*

Make certain that you have the knowledge or skill and the motivation to get the job done. For example, changing the oil and oil filter in most passenger cars is not a particularly difficult job. But, even if you are driven strongly by a desire to save money by doing the job yourself, if you lack the proper tools or dislike getting your hands smeared with black motor oil, chances are that you will postpone changing the oil as long as possible.

If you lack the knowledge for a particular job, you have several choices. First, you could change your situation by learning how to do the job. Generally, though, time pressures often prohibit your learning a particular task before its deadline. Instead, the time for proper training is before a task becomes urgent.

Second, you can delegate the task to another staff member who has the requisite knowledge for a particular task. However, while delegation can be a good time management technique, it would require that another staff member, who is properly trained for the particular task, take on additional workload.

Third, it might be possible to subcontract a particular responsibility to someone outside of the library if staff members lack the necessary expertise. Some libraries, though, would be prohibited from subcontracting work due to financial, managerial, or legal constraints.

Fourth, in some situations, it might be possible to modify or eliminate the task. For example, if you usually have a significant backlog of professional reading to do, you might reevaluate what you have selected for routing and make appropriate adjustments. There might be journals that you could drop from your reading list.

Further, library supervisors can help staff members make realistic appraisals of the task at hand to combat anxiety over possible fears of failure as well as fears of success. Staff members must know that, while library directors and supervisors do not like errors, they understand that no one is perfect. If perfection is always the minimum standard, then no one will succeed. Instead, staff members must know that most mistakes can and should be corrected and that those who strive to improve their performance will be supported, even though they make errors.

Similarly, staff members must also know that the reward for good work is not more work. While most libraries do not have the ability to provide monetary bonuses that the corporate world uses to reward good employees, supervisors can use other techniques as rewards. Above all, praise for the employee should be public, such as announcements at a staff meeting or notices in the library newsletter.

Dana Rooks in *Motivating Today's Library Staff: A Management Guide* suggests that library managers could motivate employees by helping them achieve internal rewards, such as a sense of accomplishment and higher self-esteem, as well as by providing external rewards.[23] A formal letter of acknowledgment for the employee's file and an internal achievement program might acknowledge the achievement and increase the employee's self-esteem.

3. Set aside a certain day to work on various library routines to prevent things from piling up.

Since the technical services part of a library's operations is an assembly line, allowing things to pile up creates problems both up and down the line. While scheduling regular times to work on certain library functions may not eliminate backlogs entirely, it will help keep things moving. Books requiring original cataloging, for example, frequently cause backlogs in the technical services operations of libraries of all types and sizes. Scheduling original cataloging for every Monday morning would insure that at least some of these books are cataloged each week.

Schedule some time each week for routine paperwork and reports required by the library's institution. Regular attention to paperwork prevents missed deadlines and time pressures.

4. Make a master plan.

Many people sometimes feel overwhelmed by major projects because they look at the sum of the parts, rather than the individual parts. Major library projects, such as automation, involve a large amount of planning, monitoring, and refining before they are completed. But, instead of feeling overwhelmed by the magnitude of the project, one can write a master plan for the project—including who, when, why—to get moving. Even the largest library projects begin with a plan written by some staff member, so, regardless of the size of the project, some planning will be necessary and will get the process started.

5. Divide and conquer.

Librarians and staff members can also address large projects by dividing them into smaller tasks which can be accomplished easily. For example, if your library has a backlog of books requiring original cataloging that you want to reduce, rather than taking them all on at once, set a goal for a certain number to catalog each week, or schedule a two-hour time block for one day each week to work on them.

6. Identify the worst parts of a task and focus on them first.

You may have heard the saying, "If you've got a frog to swallow, don't look at it too long." You likely will have no difficulty finding time for the easy or fun parts of the task, so concentrate first on those parts of the task that are not so appealing.

7. Carry the task around with you until you complete it.

This technique is the string-on-the-finger approach. Keeping the project before you will remind you to continue working on it. Carrying it with you also has another benefit. If you hit a time windfall, you will have the materials with you to take full advantage of it.

8. Make a public commitment to complete a task by a certain date.

If making a public commitment to meet a certain deadline will cause anxiety, then do not do it. Few people, if any at all, actually work better under pressure. However, some people find that announcing a commitment to complete a particular task by a certain time to be an effective technique because it motivates them to fulfill the commitment.

9. If you become desperate, force yourself to spend five or ten minutes each hour on the task until you get it done.

Smaller steps actually taken accomplish more than larger steps planned. By working at a task bit by bit, eventually you will get it done.

The Reality of Procrastination

People measure accomplishments in time against three standards: the past, the present, and the future. The past is gone and beyond all control, and, in this information age of rapid changes, "the future is not what it used to be."[24] That leaves people with only the present to do what must be done and accomplish their goals and objectives. So, "now is not only the best time to start, it is the only time."[25]

PAPER SHUFFLING

Many librarians are great paper shufflers, for good reason. Librarians are trained to organize and place material where it can be retrieved at some time in the future. Because that is their professional training, librarians can carry it to an extreme; paper shuffling can be a serious time management problem for librarians because it can distract staff members from the important tasks at hand. Library staff members may look busy because the papers fly from one side of the desk to the other and from the top of the pile to the bottom to the middle and then back on top, but they actually accomplish very little. Librarians should adopt several strategies to avoid the time management problems that paper shuffling causes.

One Thing at a Time

Concentrate on one task at a time. Focus all of your effort and energy on accomplishing that one task. Do not allow yourself to be distracted by other items vying for your attention. Be strict with yourself, and stay on track.

Handle Paper Only Once

Some of the greatest paper shufflers are those who pick up one item, then put it down for something else that may seem more appealing. Every time you handle an item, try to take some positive action towards its final disposition. Dropping it back into the in-box without taking some action brings you no closer to a solution; it merely adds another step until final resolution.

Some time management experts recommend the red-dot treatment for handling paper. Keep a red felt-tip pen handy, and each time you handle a report or project, mark a little red dot in the upper left corner. This provides a visual clue to move things along, particularly after the document has collected three or four red dots.

Some people cut the time necessary to reply to correspondence by writing a response on the original letter. Responding on the letter itself takes much less time than drafting a reply and having it typed, and the practice has gained such widespread acceptance that many publishers now encourage it as a means to shorten the time required to reply.

Contrary to what many may think, the computer age has not significantly lessened the problem of paper shuffling. In fact, the microcomputer has made the problem much worse. Before microcomputers, most people went to great lengths to avoid retyping documents. They corrected minor spelling errors and other mistakes in pencil or pen or with opaque fluid, and recipients of correspondence understood and accepted those practices.

But now the magic of word processing by microcomputer permits writers to change letters and other documents extremely easily, so they tend to overedit and overdraft, making inconsequential changes that add to the time required to produce a document. In the quest for absolute perfection, with the assistance of microcomputers, today's report writer may very well become a paper shuffler.

Of course, important documents must be modified as appropriate, within the limits of the time frame allowed, but ordinary reports and letters should not be overedited. For most reports, quality improves very little after more than three drafts. Most ordinary letters should not be changed substantially after two drafts, except perhaps for the correction of spelling and grammar. Regularly going beyond these limits raises the possibility that the writer is overediting the documents and should seriously question the value of the time spent in editing.

Dictate Correspondence

Dictate all correspondence. Drafting letters by hand to have them typed takes much longer and adds to the paper shuffling problem. Further, librarians who use dictation equipment that uses cassettes or microcassettes may have portable units available. Learning to use a portable dictation units will permit a librarian to take full advantage of time windfalls. Any spare moments can be converted into useful work time, almost without regard to location.

Maintain Good, Lean Files

The filing systems that librarians invent constitute another great paper-shuffling technique. As a rule, librarians are great at creating files and, as a group, probably create too many. But again this trait stems from professional training in information retrieval. Librarians are trained to file information so that it can be easily retrieved, so when deciding whether to create a new file, they, like many others in other professions, ask themselves the wrong question, Is it conceivable that we might want to refer to this again some day? The answer is nearly always yes, so they create a new file.

Instead, librarians should ask, If we want this item again and do not have it, what will we do? If the answer involves something beyond a minor inconvenience, then they should create the appropriate file. Otherwise, they should not. The purist view, espoused by many time management experts, is: When in doubt, throw it out!

One method to avoid creating files would be to install a large blackboard or bulletin board in your office to hold temporary notices. Cleanup of outdated information would be easy, and changes could be made readily.

Keeping the files in one's desk and personal office in alphabetical order saves a great deal of time. Too often, with personal files, people forget the same organization that they use for office files, forcing them to wade through all the files when they need to find information in a hurry. Instead, eliminate that hassle simply by keeping those files, too, in alphabetical order.

Several experts in time management recommend keeping a "hold" or "action" file near your desk for items that will require action within the next several days but require no action now. So, rather than file it in the permanent files only to have to retrieve and then refile it, wait until you have acted before placing it in the permanent files. Chances are good that, after you have acted on the item, you will not need it again for some time.

Obviously, a hold file would contain items needed to perform work related to items appearing on your list of priority tasks. Keeping these items close at hand will assist in the efficient completion of the priority tasks and, thus, encourage you to focus on those items.

Keep filing in the library's permanent records up to date. Depending on the size of your library, you may not need to file every day, but you should probably file at least once a week to keep clutter from accumulating.

Keep a Neat Desk

A cluttered desk holds many potential interruptions. Despite how disciplined you are, the stacks of paper on a cluttered desk can form a major distraction. To keep focused on one project at a time, your desk should be clear of all other papers.

The ability to keep a neat desk operates according to a very simple principle: output must equal input. If input exceeds output, your desk will be cluttered. Monitor the level of your in-box frequently throughout the day, and try to keep items from accumulating. Use a vertical sorting file as a holding file for low priority materials waiting for your attention and to control the flow of papers onto your desk.

Clear everything off your desk but the project at hand. If your office is large enough, place a credenza behind your desk to hold basic desk items like a stapler, tape dispenser, and other necessities. Getting those items off your desk will clear more work space.

Always know what is on your desk. Unidentified piles of papers create delays, particularly when you need to find something in a hurry.

Rearrange your in-box and out-box to flow more naturally with your style. If you are right-handed, you should probably place your in-box on the right side of your desk and your out-box on the left. If you are left-handed, try the reverse.

Clean off your desk regularly. Desks are work tools; they need to be cleaned regularly to prevent breakdowns. Pick a day like the first Friday of every month to get down to the bare surface. If your desk is now cluttered, you may be tempted to take a shovel and clear your desk quite abruptly. Resist the temptation to act rashly, and, instead, locate four small boxes, the size depending on the amount of clutter on your desk. The larger the amount of clutter on the desk, the larger the boxes that you will need.

Label the boxes "Priority," "Routine," "Junk Mail," and "Reading," and sort all of the clutter on your desk into the boxes. Papers relating to high-priority items obviously go into the Priority box. Place materials for low-priority items into the Routine box. Journals and other professional reading go into the Reading box, and you know what goes into the Junk-Mail box. Work quickly, and do not study any item long. If this part of the cleanup drags on, it means that you are reading more than you are sorting.

Once you have sorted all of the material, and your desk is clean again, start working on the items in the Priority box. Employ the techniques of uninterrupted time for concentrated work and of handling paperwork efficiently to reduce the pile in the box.

Handle the other items after you have scheduled time to deal with the high-priority things. Place the items from the Routine box in a vertical holding file or similar place for disposition later. Similarly, the items from the Reading box should go in your time windfall file for reading while you are waiting for appointments or while you are traveling.

Sort the Mail

One important way to stay on top of the paper pile involves properly sorting the mail. If a secretary handles incoming mail for the library, provide the following guidelines about sorting.

First, separate the first-class, library-rate, and book-rate mail from the bulk-rate mail. Since book ads usually come by bulk rate, most of the items in this category can be handled easily. Place all book ads in a folder or box to be handled once each week. You may find that such a pile accumulates in a week that you need a small mail cart to handle them.

Second, refer the library-rate and book-rate items to the appropriate departments for handling. Library-rate mail often involves interlibrary loans, and book-rate items usually go to the acquisitions department.

Open and sort the first-class mail into folders, one for important mail—the priority items—and one for routine matters. Your secretary may need training to spot priority items since libraries receive such a large volume of mail on a daily basis. Some librarians may prefer to sort their mail themselves to keep something important from being mishandled, but you should delegate this task whenever possible.

As you handle incoming mail and memos, following a simple strategy will help you stay on top of the mountain of paper. Place a trash can next to the library mailboxes and scan your incoming mail there. Toss immediately all mail and memos for which you have no use; do not bring these into your office.

Refer letters and memos to other library staff members as appropriate. Do not let something that should be referred sit in your in-box for several days before passing it on. Refer it when you first scan the mail.

Simplify Paperwork

Reducing the paperwork at your library will ease the paper-shuffling problem. First, question seriously whether you need to route materials to someone else on the staff, with only the designation "For Your Information." Unless you know that the individual needs to see the material, resist the impulse to send it out just because she *might* find it useful. Be certain. You probably receive more from your colleagues now than you care to read, so be considerate of others.

Second, limit the number of photocopies that you make of any report, letter, or memo. If you know that additional copies of a report will be needed in the future but are not sure how many copies you will need, keep one copy with a cover sheet labeled Master from which all other copies will be made. If the report is long and you are likely to need a copy quickly, keep one copy for distribution. Do not make others until you need them.

Making and keeping copies that you never use adds unnecessarily to the bulk of your library files. This just creates a weeding task for you or for the library secretary in the future. So, maintaining adequate, but lean, files will save you time overall.

Third, evaluate whether the reports and forms that your library uses are really necessary, particularly if the library is automated. Reports tend to become immortal. That is, they frequently outlive their usefulness, but staff members continue to produce them as part of an established routine. Library administrators should reevaluate all periodic reports at least annually to insure that these reports continue to serve a useful purpose.

Fourth, streamline procedures by eliminating duplicate record keeping. This may appear to be a problem limited chiefly to library systems with branch libraries where duplicate serials records as well as others are kept. But even small libraries can keep duplicate records, perhaps even unknowingly. For example, some libraries may keep two sets of binding records, one with the serials records and the other with the staff member responsible for preparing bindery shipments. One set kept with the serial records should suffice in most library situations.

Use a Microcomputer

If you use a microcomputer daily, you might consider using one of several database management programs to relieve the clutter of paper on your desk. If most of the information that you need to track is structured, that is, able to be categorized, you can use a standard flat-file database management program, such as Professional File,[26] Q&A,[27] or PC-File Plus.[28]

Several good, inexpensive flat-file database management programs exist, but, as with many other things, you get what you pay for with these programs. With the inexpensive programs you must anticipate most of your needs fairly accurately for categories as well as for the maximum length of each entry because, generally speaking, you cannot adjust them easily afterwards.

If your information varies considerably, such as notes for a memo or report, figures for long-range shelving needs, and the names and addresses of several barcode vendors, you need a free-form database management program, such as AskSam,[29] InfoXL,[30] Lotus Agenda,[31] Tornado,[32] or Zyindex.[33] These provide more flexibility, but, consequently, they can cost more than flat-file programs and be more difficult to learn and use.

FIGHT PREOCCUPATION

Preoccupation, or daydreaming, distracts one from completing priority tasks. Fight preoccupation by taking regular breaks, even naps, for refreshment. Public services staff members often skip breaks because of the constant urgencies of the job, but library directors and those who supervise library staff members should be mindful of this and encourage public services staff to take breaks as they can.

Many executives use a simple technique to stay focused on hard work. They take a five-minute break each hour to fight fatigue. During the break, they get up and move around the office to break the effects of preoccupation.

Physical conditioning plays an important role in fighting preoccupation, too. Regular exercise helps to keep your mind sharp and gives you the stamina to handle the day. Many top executives insist that their employees get regular exercise, reasoning that people too busy to exercise cannot give the organization their best work efforts.

You need not undertake a full workout to fight the effects of preoccupation, though. Take advantage of the necessity to move about. When you walk to another person's office, walk briskly. Use the stairs when possible, not the elevator. The physical motion will help fight off a sluggish, tired feeling.

One nonphysical way to fight the effects of preoccupation, though, is to record ideas as you have them. Keep pencil and paper ready in your car, at home by your bed, and in a drawer at your desk in the office. Some executives also carry a portable dictation unit with them so that they can record ideas conveniently. Librarians can use this technique at professional conferences, for example, when visiting the exhibit areas. By recording notes on new products or reminders to talk to specific vendors, librarians at a conference need not worry about relying on their memories to pursue their good ideas.

PERFECTIONISM

The problem of perfectionism poses a great time management challenge to librarians. Time management theorists decry the high cost of perfectionism for both people and organizations. Very few things, if any, are truly perfect, so, if librarians expect perfection and require it as a minimum standard, they will often be disappointed in their own job performance and in their staff members' performance.

In addition, many librarians may strive for perfection out of fear of failure and criticism. After all, who can criticize perfection? But, high achievers realize that excellence is close enough to perfection with most things.

However, a competing reality is that a library is not like many other operations in that it relies heavily on detail. Librarians must insist on precision in certain aspects of library operation. For example, a book whose spine label has just two numbers reversed might be misshelved and effectively lost in a large collection because library users cannot find it.

A reasonable approach for librarians would be to design and maintain methods of double-checking for those library operations where even simple errors would cost much in time and frustration later on. Most libraries, for example, already provide for routine checks for new books processed to insure that spine labels and book pockets are correct.

ATTENTION TO LIBRARY ROUTINES

Librarians must also consider the assembly-line nature of library operations when planning time management strategies. Particularly with acquisitions, cataloging, processing, and shelving, library operations resemble a manufacturer's assembly line. Consequently, backlogs in one part of the line will idle staff members further down and will slow workers above the backlog as well. Further, backlogs in the line directly affect the ability of the public services staff to give good reference service. Library services suffer if the reference source needed now is still in cataloging, for example. Librarians must pay regular attention to routines as good time management.

THE MYTH OF WORKING UNDER PRESSURE

Nearly everyone knows someone who claims to work better under pressure, and perhaps someone, somewhere, does. However, most librarians working under pressure take on the mad-whirl appearance of the "Frazzled Librarian" described by Andrew Berner.[34]

Studies tend to support the claim that people do not work better under pressure. In *Working Under Pressure*, Vernon E. Buck reviewed psychological and sociological studies of managers and workers and concluded that "the quality and quantity of production was no greater for managers and workers who were under pressure than for those who weren't. In fact, the trend was towards perceptions of job pressure being associated with inferior production records."[35] Buck concluded from his review that managers who felt under pressure were less enthusiastic, less happy and less satisfied with their jobs than those who felt that they were not under pressure.

In one sense, though, many people like working under pressure because they can blame failures or poor quality on the lack of time—I did my best in the time available. But, all too often, their own procrastination created the time pressure, so the excuse lacks merit.

CRISIS MANAGEMENT

Of course, unforeseen crises may create time pressure. The best time management strategy for a crisis is to cope as well as possible and to learn what can be done to prevent reoccurrences.

During a crisis, one should not attempt to delegate a task to a library staff member if that person has not been properly trained beforehand. Improper delegation will only exacerbate the crisis. Instead, one must endure the crisis however is best and resolve to prevent the crisis from reoccurring.

Following the crisis, conduct a study to determine why the crisis occurred, then make changes, if possible, to correct any problems. If you control what you can, you will have more time to cope with what you cannot control.

STRESS REDUCTION AND BURNOUT

Stress in library staff members can build from several different sources, some within the control of library directors and supervisors and some beyond their control. Working under pressure causes stress, which seriously affects the quality of work, and poor quality work wastes time because of the errors made that must be corrected.

Some library staff members experience stress when they work closely with other people. A coworker with irritating mannerisms, prejudices, or poor work habits can cause stress to build over a period of time. Obviously, staff members must work closely in most library situations, so stress may result and be a problem in some libraries. Encourage staff members in their work through compliments made in public and by jokes told at break time and help build morale by scheduling fun activities occasionally, like a library picnic or a party.

Other staff members experience stress when working with the public. Demanding, sometimes rude, and inconsiderate library users can create

stressful situations. Using a quiet voice and giving calm, careful expla-
nations may soothe the library user and thus reduce the amount of stress
that the situation has created.

Sometimes, external factors create stressful working conditions. Inadequate ventilation, a poorly designed physical plant, as well as the
policies and procedures of the institution may be the cause of stress in
library staff members. For example, if your library experiences budget
cuts, you can expect to see the effects of stress in the library staff,
particularly if the cuts include personnel. Some concerns can be addressed through good communications and adjustments in library policies, but some matters may be largely beyond the control of library
directors and those who supervise library staff members. In those
situations, library directors must provide honest information about the
financial situation of the institution to the staff.

Stress can also result from internal factors that library directors and
those who supervise library staff members have absolutely no control
over. Marital problems, legal difficulties, or severe financial strains may
create stress. The institution in which the library is located may provide
professional counseling or referrals to outside aid, and the employee
should be encouraged to take advantage of these opportunities.

Besides outside help, stress can be relieved through the pursuit of
non-work-related activities as well. Regular exercise and other good
health habits such as eating a proper diet and taking regular breaks can
reduce stress. In addition, you can relieve personal stress through a
complete change of scenery and concentration. Refresh yourself with
your hobbies, or take a vacation.

In addition, you can prevent some of the effects of stress by adopting
a good sense of humor. Learn not to take things, including yourself, too
seriously. According to some, libraries tend to be not very humorous
places, so you may face quite a challenge.[36]

Ultimately, of course, stress can lead to the condition known as
burnout. Burnout differs from stress in that it typically centers on
job-related activities, while stress affects both work and personal activities.

Burnout is a condition common to the service profession and is
characterized by physical, emotional, and behavioral symptoms. Physical
symptoms include tense neck and shoulder muscles and recurring
problems with colds and headaches, among others. Emotional symptoms
include moodiness and overwhelming mental exhaustion. And, behavioral symptoms appear as impersonal treatment of library users, un-
flattering characterization of library users, tardiness, and absenteeism.[37]

Researchers have identified candidates for burnout as those who are highly motivated, idealistic people who try to attain impossible goals;[38] further studies have shown that librarians generally may be at risk for burnout.[39] In recent surveys, directors of academic, state, public, and special libraries report that taking on too much work at once is one of their most serious time management problems,[40] and Woodsworth asserts that a high turnover rate among library directors evidences burnout.[41] Accepting these as two causes of burnout, it appears that, while librarians may be at risk overall, perhaps at least one group of library directors suffers less from burnout than other groups of directors. A recent survey of academic law library directors indicated that mobility among these directors was much less than suspected, with most directors still in their first or second directorship.[42]

POSITIVE OUTLOOK

One of the most important techniques in time management for librarians is having a positive outlook on work. A positive outlook gives you motivation to practice good time management. At the end of the day, look back at the things that you accomplished, rather than those still left to do. Focus on the books cataloged or reference questions answered rather than the backlogs awaiting you.

TIME FOR PROFESSIONAL DEVELOPMENT

Every person who enters the library profession and remains a librarian does so for some reason of personal satisfaction. Some aspect of the profession provides particular individual enjoyment and gratification. Each librarian needs to recognize the source of this fulfillment, to plan for activities that keep that professional spark alive.

Obviously, for librarians to remain satisfied with their choice of career, they must continually nurture those aspects of the profession that convinced them to become librarians. Otherwise, librarians can lose the creative interest that brought them to the profession. To some extent, librarians share this kind of problem with members of other professions. The men and women of the clergy, for example, sometimes become so caught up in being the spiritual leaders for others that they fail to take time for personal spiritual growth.

In much the same way, librarians must nurture themselves as professionals. This nurturance can be somewhat of a challenge to some librarians, particularly those who move into library administration. As they become library administrators, they find frequently that their job duties change so much that they no longer are actively involved in the kind of library work that may have attracted them to the profession initially. And, if they do not find the same kind of personal satisfaction with their new duties, difficulties in motivation may arise.

For a librarian who no longer feels fulfilled by the kind of professional duties that a new position has, the solution to finding personal satisfaction in the job may not be easy. Job responsibilities in a library can differ significantly, and the real challenge for this librarian as well as for the supervisor will be to find the appropriate combination of duties to provide both personal satisfaction and smooth, effective library operation.

One aspect of continuing professional growth, of course, is involvement in library association activities. If a librarian has a goal of achieving a level of success in the library profession, she should develop a strategy to become involved in the leadership of the profession. Too often, some librarians give the lowest priority to those activities designed to increase professional development when assigning priorities on a daily basis. The cumulative effect of assigning low priority to professional development activities is that these librarians achieve far less than others. If a librarian places a high value on achievement in the library profession, and the library's institution supports that as well, then she must plan to spend time regularly in broader professional activities, rather than continually postponing them for the sake of convenience.

3

Time Management
Techniques Involving Others

On first consideration, one might think that effective time management
is entirely personal in nature, and it is true that successful time management depends on personal motivation. But, effective time management
for a librarian must include techniques for dealing with other people.
After all, the concept of a library requires, by definition, a community
of users—the faculty and students of a college or university, the citizens
of a town, city, or county, or the employees at a corporation or other
business. Since a librarian serves a community of library users, her work
habits necessarily involve other people, so techniques designed to
improve the librarian's performance should include ones that consider
interaction with other people, as well.

This chapter also includes techniques and considerations for librarians
to use in working with other library staff members. Techniques normally
used by library administrators, such as delegation, are included in the
following chapter.

THE NATURE OF LIBRARY OPERATIONS

Librarians in one-person shops know all too well the many hats that
they must wear to make their libraries successful. While virtually all of
those operations take place on a grander scale in larger libraries, the
sheer size of those libraries and the numbers of the clientele that they
serve force specialization on the staff. And, while specialization permits
staff members to develop considerable expertise in one facet of library

operations, it also fosters a sense of compartmentalization of the library staff. That is, library staff members in large libraries sometimes know little about how their particular departments contribute to the overall operation of the library.

To combat the bad effects of compartmentalization, many libraries prepare extensive orientation programs for new professional and support staff members. Each new staff member spends time in each department of the library observing and learning the operation. Department heads must be committed to such a program because it requires detailed coordination between departments to be successful, and it delays the day when a new staff member will be at her post full-time. But, the cost is small compared to what the new staff member can then contribute to the library.

In many libraries, special projects present themselves periodically. Librarians should take great care in planning special projects to avoid having to undo them later. One strategy is to include staff members from all departments in planning the projects so that potential problems will not be overlooked.

Occasionally, but certainly more often than most librarians would like, backlogs occur in some area of library operations. Librarians in middle management must be alert to problems such as these and bring them to the attention of the library director for appropriate action. Resolving problems before they develop into major crises promotes good time management.

INTERRUPTIONS

Interruptions provide one of the biggest challenges to librarians; recent studies report that directors of all types of libraries identify drop-in visitors as one of their most serious time management problems.[1] A typical librarian's day often consists of one interruption after another by coworkers, library administrators, and clientele. There never seems to be enough time, money, or personnel to get everything accomplished. Librarians as managers, it seems, are not substantially different from other managers in experiencing interruption. According to a recent study, the average manager is interrupted every eight minutes.[2] So it should come as no surprise that an important part of time management involves controlling interruptions.

In a way, a librarian's own desire to be helpful to library users contributes to the problems of interruptions. Contemporary library philosophy encourages librarians to be accessible to library users, so librarians give up time readily to almost anyone who asks "just a quick question."

Librarians, perhaps more than most other professionals, are subject to more interruptions because much of their work is "invisible." Even professionals whose work depends heavily on support from libraries, like attorneys, have little idea of what librarians do and, worse, perpetuate the misconceptions. One attorney, while attempting the worthy cause of encouraging law firms to hire librarians, described one of the essential qualifications for librarians as "a love of books."[3]

While some librarians are undoubtedly bibliophiles, that should be a matter of personal choice, not a job requirement. Being a bibliophile does not provide assurance of success as a librarian, and the reverse is very true: many successful librarians are not bibliophiles.

This lack of understanding the duties of a librarian encourages interruptions. Because many people have the mistaken belief that librarians do little but read all day, they also believe that librarians have no other requests than theirs competing for time and attention.

Librarians can use many techniques to deal with interruptions. Some techniques discourage or prevent interruptions. Others help librarians cope with interruptions to lessen their sometimes disastrous effects.

Whether librarians should work actively to discourage or prevent interruptions deserves some serious consideration. After all, most employers hire librarians to organize a collection of information for use and to assist some client group in using that collection. So, if the clientele of the library interrupt frequently with requests for assistance, then the employers may view that as nothing more than the librarian doing his job.

On the other hand, practical necessity in most situations forces librarians to cope with competing demands on their time and to complete some tasks before accepting new ones. Handling interruptions effectively can provide them with the time necessary to complete one task before moving to a new one.

1. Remember that a librarian's job consists of interruptions.

Nearly every librarian, late on a Friday afternoon, has been asked at least one tough reference question from an unpleasant library user or received a "rush" project from the library director that caused her to question her career choice.

When faced with that kind of situation, one would do well to recall that a librarian's job is to deal with a near constant influx of information, material, and demands for assistance, and interruptions come with the territory. Accepting the reality in which a library operates is one important means of coping with interruptions.

2. Anticipate the request.

Prepare library guides or handouts that will answer the most common questions. Library guides and handouts that show the general layout of the collection, the location of restrooms and water fountains, and other important information from the user's point of view will prevent a lot of interruptions. In this day of desktop publishing, more libraries can afford to produce very attractive publications and keep them current. Obviously, providing good resources for the staff at the reference desk, too, will shorten the time required for routine requests.

3. Close your office door.

The most effective way to limit interruptions is to close your office door, despite how that might contradict the contemporary library philosophy of wanting to project an open and inviting image. If you are concerned that your closed office door might project the wrong image, compromise. Close your door during your concentrated work time only for part of the day or for certain days of the week.

Further, placing a "Do Not Disturb—At Work" sign on your office door will let staff and library users know that you are isolating yourself to concentrate on important work. If that seems too offensive, try a simple sign, "Please Knock," posted at eye level on the door. Staff members and library users with important questions will continue to seek your advice, but the sign may postpone some interruptions for less important matters.

A library administrator might also develop a code of sorts with other library staff members. Closing the door completely could mean not to disturb her. A partially open door could mean to disturb her only for important non-routine matters. A completely open door could mean that she was available for questions of any kind.

Whatever method you choose involving your office, discuss it first with the library staff members who report to you so that they know the system as well as the reasons for it.

4. Rearrange your office furniture to discourage casual conversation from passersby.

If your desk is located such that people can see you as they walk by, chances are that they will interrupt you more often than if your back is to them. Most people will pause to speak to someone, particularly a coworker, when they walk by. But, one small word often expands quickly into a distracting conversation that can keep you from finishing the important task on which you are working. Although it may appear to be rude, turning your back on other library staff will limit interruptions.

5. Stack papers or books in the chairs in your office to discourage visitors from sitting.

Generally, people will not sit down uninvited if they have to move a stack of papers. However, you may want to use this technique only during your periods of concentrated work when you do not want to be disturbed. Otherwise, the stacked papers will add clutter to the office and might cause a time management problem in itself.

6. Use nonverbal clues to discourage long interruptions.

Stand up when someone enters your office and do not sit down unless you want that person to interrupt you. Most people entering an office will not sit unless they are invited to do so if the person in the office is standing. Better, you could meet visitors outside of the office and talk standing up.

If you are caught sitting when someone enters your office, stand up to end the conversation at the appropriate time and start walking to the door. Again, most people will stand and walk to the door with you. These techniques provide the visual clues that you do not want to prolong the interruption.

7. Use verbal clues to discourage long interruptions.

You can also use a number of verbal clues to indicate to a visitor that you want to keep the visit short. As the person enters the room, to set the expectation that the visit will be short, say something like, I won't invite you to sit down, It will save your time and mine.

Be honest about time limits. Saying, Two minutes is about all I have to spare right now, I'm working on a big project that must get out today, gives notice to the visitor to get to the point quickly. Finally, to bring things to a close, summarize the conversation and say something like, I guess that sums it up. The visitor then will likely take the verbal clue and leave.

8. Use planned interruptions to keep other interruptions short.

Planned interruptions can be a technique to shorten other interruptions. If you have a meeting scheduled with a known time waster, before the person arrives, ask your secretary or another staff member to call or knock on the door after about fifteen minutes to remind you to prepare for another appointment. The other appointment can be imaginary, but the technique helps move the first meeting to a close.

Some librarians feel uncomfortable using imaginary appointments to limit interruptions. Say instead, I have other matters on my schedule today that I must attend to now. That provides the closure to the conversation without a lie, since your work and appointment schedule and list of priority tasks most likely contains other items vying for your attention.

9. Be honest about when you can get to a client's request.

Remember that a librarian's workload is largely invisible to clients, so they do not know what else you have to do unless you tell them. After you have explained the situation, move to complete the highest-ranked priority task. Do not engage in conversation pertaining to social matters if other matters are pressing. That only reinforces the notion that librarians do not have much work to do.

10. Provide some time each day for concentrated work for each staff member who reports to you.

Everyone needs some uninterrupted time each day, but all too often library directors and other library supervisors overlook this. Instead, they expect all staff members to be "on call" throughout the day. Worse, some library staff members do not have adequate work space, such as a private office. No one can expect to do concentrated work at the reference desk or next to the cataloging computer terminal.

11. Cooperate with coworkers in being on call to allow each some time with limited interruptions.

Each staff member should cooperate with coworkers in being on call, to the greatest extent possible, to allow each some time with limited interruptions.

12. Limit your interruptions of other staff members.

If you do not want to be interrupted frequently, do not interrupt other staff members. Instead, save interruptions for important problems and batch the small stuff to handle at one time.

13. Use hideaways.

If your library has a conference room, you might be able to use that as a workplace to limit interruptions. If your library has empty office space, convert it for others' temporary use. Even the desk of someone who is on vacation might be enough of a hideaway. If your library has carrels, consider using one when you need to complete a major project.

For hideaways to be effective, though, all staff members must know and respect the basic ground rule: Do not interrupt anyone working in a different office or at a different desk.

14. Train staff members to scrutinize their interruptions.

Before interrupting another staff member, each person should analyze her question. First, if it can be answered by referring to written library policies or procedures, those sources should be consulted before interrupting anyone.

Second, if someone less busy can answer the question, that person should be the one to ask. Other staff members besides the director, for example, may have the institutional memory or knowledge to answer a particular question.

Third, the question might concern something that only one person in the library can handle, but it might not require a face-to-face interruption. Consider using a short note, the intercom, or the telephone for those questions that can be answered quickly.

15. Do not lose your train of thought.

Limit the effects of interruptions so that you do not lose your train of thought. Always carry notepaper or a small spiral book with you when walking in the library to take notes of other requests made when people stop you.

COMMUNICATIONS

Good time management involving other people depends on good communications. Misunderstandings and twisted communications take time to straighten out. If communications are clear in the first place, no clarification or correction is necessary, and time is not wasted.

Indeed, the directors of special libraries report that one of their most serious time management problems is inadequate, inaccurate, or delayed information.[4] Maintaining good communication skills would limit problems here, both in transmitting and receiving information. Librarians must use good communication skills in reference interviews to determine what information the library user really needs. Further, they must use good communication skills in receiving assignments from superiors and from coworkers so that their reports will contain the information requested in time for it to be of the greatest value.

Good communicators will use a variety of means to maintain good communications with staff and coworkers, including contact in informal settings. Consider taking breaks occasionally with other library staff members and use other means, such as celebrating staff members' birthdays, to build morale and support good communications.

Though some staff members may view this as a bit impersonal, keep note cards handy to provide a means for quick communication. Obviously, you will not want to rely primarily on notes as the chief means of communication with staff and coworkers, but sending short notes can be effective in saving time, particularly in larger libraries or those where the staff is not centrally located.

Sometimes, though, library staff members carry memo-writing to an extreme. When library directors and those who supervise library staff members see a situation develop round by round through memos, they should stop the cycle before it escalates into a major problem and call a staff meeting to resolve the difficulties. Some situations, particularly personnel conflicts, require meetings; they cannot be resolved through a series of memos.

Communicate clearly about deadlines. Some library directors and supervisors set phantom deadlines for staff members to insure that needed information is available before their final deadline, and this can be a successful technique. However, if staff members learn the real deadline for their work, the end result may not be significantly different.

Further, never use ASAP as a deadline. While it may have meant "as soon as possible" once, it now means "when it is convenient." Instead, establish a definite deadline.

Another effective technique is to involve all of the participants in a project when setting a deadline. Getting input from the staff members affected by a deadline may reveal the need to assign a new lower priority to a current project. Staff members may need to delay working on one project to meet the new project's deadline.

When a deadline has been negotiated, ask each staff member affected, Do I have your word on it? Participating in setting the deadline helps insure some commitment on the part of library staff members, but they are much more likely to meet those deadlines for which they have made a direct verbal commitment to a supervisor.

In much the same manner, librarians must communicate clearly with clientele concerning any delivery deadlines for the information requested. Obviously, providing good library service requires delivering the information requested within the necessary time frame for the library user to utilize it effectively.

At the same time, librarians must insure that the information provided to the user is what, in fact, the user needs. As reference librarians know all too well, what library users ask for is often not what they really need, so the reference interview figures prominently in library service and consequently has become a standard part of library education.[5] In fact, different styles of interviewing have been studied, each with its own merits, designed to provide good communications between librarian and library user.[6]

Effective communication between library departments also supports good time management. Figure 3.1 shows a form that one library uses for each book added to the collection to alert departments to any special procedures.

MEETINGS

Meetings often waste everyone's time because they are called unnecessarily, the participants fail to prepare adequately, and the moderators fail to keep discussion relevant. Few librarians learn in library school how to run an effective meeting, but meetings constitute a significant portion of most librarians' time at work. Because of that, research indicates that meetings comprise one of the largest time management problems for librarians.[7]

While some time management experts recommend categorically not to call meetings or attend them, realistically, most librarians cannot follow that advice strictly.

Most librarians must attend meetings regularly for a variety of reasons. First, of course, your supervisor may require your attendance. Staff meetings called by the library director, for example, would be difficult to miss.

Figure 3.1
Cataloging/Processing Slip

ACQUISTIONS/SERIALS
____RUSH ORDER; NOTIFY_____

____FACULTY REQUEST _____

RARE, NO MARKS!

____Make Serials Record

____Change SR Source _____

____Routing _____

____SR Note _____

____Frequency/Change _____

____Cancel Order ____Return

____Enter Standing Order

____Copy # ____

CATALOGING
___Micro___A/V___Ref.___Reserve

____Rare Book___Classified

____Other Location _____

____New Ed. ____Earlier Ed.

____Recat. _____

____Withdraw _____

__Cat.&Class sep.__Trace Series

____Open entry

__Return catalog info. to
Serial Record

____049 field _____

____090/099 fields _____

___590 field ___Latest on Ref.

____Latest Only kept _____

____Title Changed-was: _____

____Ceased w/ _____

____Continued by _____

____Close entry _____

____Gift ____Donor _____

PROCESSING
____DO NOT REMOVE

__Bind __Box / current issues

____Latest at _____

____Move others to Classified

____Discard superseded
issues/vol./ed.

____Correct ____Repair

____Bind. rec. ___Freq.____

____Route to _____

____Make Shelf Dummy

CIRCULATION
____Note filing/shelving
instruc.

____Check out to _____

____Add to/delete from Library

Publications: _____

____Course Reserve _____

REFERENCE
____Notify _____

____Acquisitions List

____New Reference Book

____Suggest Location

Second, you might need to attend a meeting to get correct information for handling a particular situation. In a crisis, for example, it may be necessary to distribute information to the staff as a group so that everyone gets the same information at the same time.

Third, if you are involved directly with the goal of the meeting, you should attend, of course. Groups assigned with the planning and implementation of library projects such as automation must meet regularly to keep the project moving smoothly.

Fourth, the politics of your job may require you to attend certain meetings. Increasingly, librarians work to develop good public relations for their libraries, and this may require the presence of the librarians at certain meetings.

Calling a Meeting

Librarians can minimize the time-wasting effects of any meetings that they call by using the following techniques.

1. Weigh the options and consider alternatives.

If you intend only to disseminate information, you might be able to use a memo more effectively. If you seek opinions or discussion, consider alternatives such as a telephone conference call, electronic mail, or a video conference.

To aid in making the decision whether to call a meeting, project some of the costs by adding up salary time. Viewed that way, you might be surprised to see how expensive even a small meeting can be.

2. Hold the meeting standing up.

Standing speeds almost any meeting along, and you need no special physical arrangements. Staff meetings held in a hallway or while standing in the library director's office can be more effective than traditional meetings because the participants tend to avoid irrelevant discussion. Quick meetings needed for clarification of problems are an excellent choice in which to use this technique.

3. Establish a definite beginning time and a suggested ending time.

The person who calls the meeting establishes the norm for punctuality. If you routinely begin five minutes late, soon every participant will know that punctuality means being five minutes late to each of your meetings.

No one likes to be kept waiting, so common courtesy requires that you begin each meeting on time.

Also, set a general time limit to provide both an incentive to keep to the point and a reward for attending the meeting. Realistic time limits help the participants plan their own daily schedules better.

In setting the time limit, be aware of the fatigue factor that diminishes the value of the meeting. Some librarians, for example, hold steadfastly to a maximum time limit of 30 minutes for all library staff meetings. While that limit might be a bit too short, no staff meeting should be allowed to continue on aimlessly, and experience may suggest an appropriate limit.

Unless the meeting requires maximum concentration from all the participants, schedule the meeting for the late afternoon. The closer the meeting is to quitting time, the less likely participants will be to stray from the subject.

4. Send an agenda to the participants beforehand,
including an estimate of the time for each item.

If someone is assigned to report at the meeting, make sure that she is ready to do it. If a major report will not be ready in time, either cancel the meeting or delete that item from the agenda. Librarians respect the value of information in the decision-making process, so librarians would do themselves an injustice to allow discussion and decisions made in their own meetings based on incomplete information.

5. Review the physical arrangements for the meeting
beforehand.

The larger the meeting, the more important it is that one check the physical arrangements beforehand. Large meetings tend to be more formal, and members of larger groups resent wasting time while waiting for the room to be set up properly. Be certain that the room is large enough and set up as you requested with more than enough chairs and with any special audiovisual equipment in place.

6. Keep the meeting moving.

Each meeting should have a person designated for one of three functions: a moderator, a timekeeper, and a recorder. In small meetings, one person may be able to handle more than one function, but, in larger meetings, only one function should be assigned to a particular person.

Generally, if you called the meeting, you will serve as moderator. The moderator must take an active role in conducting the meeting. A good moderator will always ask speakers to relate their comments to the subject of discussion if those comments seem to be irrelevant. In one sense, the moderator guides the meeting by adhering to the established agenda.

On the other hand, the moderator should be careful not to stifle creativity and enthusiasm. Some of the best ideas come from the interaction of a group of people, so a meeting can be a good source of creative ideas if the moderator allows sufficient latitude. Above all, do not end a meeting solely to conform to the suggested time limit if discussion continues and progresses towards the resolution of the issues facing the group.

If you serve as timekeeper, as the title implies, you watch the clock. Prompt the moderator quietly when the allocated time expires for each agenda item. The moderator or the group itself may then decide to extend the time limit for discussion of that item.

The recorder at a meeting takes detailed notes of any actions taken, particularly of any assignments made for subsequent meetings. Shortly after the meeting, the recorder circulates to all participants the written record so that any misunderstandings can be resolved while the meeting is still fresh in everyone's minds. All assignments to participants of the meeting must be clear so that the individuals responsible for further action can complete their assignment well before any subsequent meetings.

When further investigation is needed, appoint a committee to collect the information and make recommendations later. Do not waste everyone's time in discussing a matter which cannot be resolved.

7. Allow participants to leave during the meeting if they are not needed anymore.

While this demonstrates respect for everyone's time, logistics and propriety may prevent the moderator from allowing participants to leave certain meetings.

8. Adjourn the meeting and reconvene the next day if necessary to break a deadlock.

If the meeting deadlocks because two or more major camps develop, consider adjourning the meeting to allow for personal reflection, rather than letting the meeting drag on if no progress appears likely. After considering the matter overnight, the participants in the major camps may take more conciliatory positions.

9. Summarize comments throughout the meeting.

This facilitates note taking for both the recorder and the participants, as well as promotes understanding. Before you adjourn, make sure that everyone understands what decisions were reached and what duties everyone has, if any, to collect and distribute information for the next meeting.

Use a simple grid, such as that in Figure 3.2, to record the agenda items from the meeting, the action taken, and notes on any continuing responsibilities.

10. Be realistic about the number of agenda items for the meeting.

Do not attempt to take on too much at any meeting. Be aware that a fatigue factor may set in that can diminish the amount of work done. Tired participants may be inclined to agree too easily just to end the meeting, rather than giving the agenda items the attention that they deserve.

11. Invite the right number of people.

As the number of people participating in the meeting grows, the amount of detailed work that can be accomplished shrinks correspondingly. Larger meetings are appropriate for matters such as disseminating information and broad approval of operating policy. The participants in smaller meetings can accomplish detailed drafting of proposals and policies. Generally, invite no more than three to five participants for a meeting where detailed work will be the main agenda item.

12. Avoid serving food.

Serving food, even pastries and coffee, at a meeting adds to its length. Further, serving food complicates the logistical problems in preparing for the meeting.

Attending a Meeting

Everyone who participates in a meeting plays an active role in its success or failure. Participants should follow these guidelines for every meeting.

Figure 3.2
Decision Grid

Agenda Item	Action	Comments	Responsible
Circulation Policy changes	Postponed	Consider different classes of materials	John to collect statistics on bound journals
Automation Project progress report	Information only	Barcoding taking longer than estimated	Cathy to contact Friends group for volunteers
Telefacsimile policy for library users	Adopted with changes	Increased fee to transmit to $1.50 per page for domestic calls	Carol to make sign for bulletin board
Plans to host meeting of metro area library association	Discussion only	Conducting tours of library, program on library services and special collections	George to contact Friends group for volunteers
Employee evaluations	Information only	All employees to be evaluated during March	Julie will distribute forms and procedures by Feb. 15
Professional librarians' activity reports	Information only	Change this year in reporting book reviews in library journals; deadline Feb. 15	Julie will distribute revised forms by Feb. 1

1. Prepare for the meeting by reading the materials distributed.

Your role as an informed participant is just as important to the success of the meeting as the moderator's. Study the materials well in advance of the meeting so that you can ask questions that will resolve any uncertainties that you have. If the author of the materials is available, ask your questions before the meeting begins so that you save more time.

2. Stay on course.

Resist the temptation to go off on tangents, and encourage others to stick to the business at hand. Although, at the same time, do not be dissuaded from thinking creatively about the item under discussion. That may lead you into other topics not strictly relevant to the original item, but, if you and the other participants are making good use of the time, then the group most likely will not object to the momentary divergence.

3. Take along other reading or work.

If you must attend a regular meeting that frequently wastes your time, you might be able to get other work done there, if you do it discreetly.

LEARNING TO SAY NO

Librarians tend to be some of the most over-committed service professionals, for good reason. After all, a librarian serves the information needs of the library's clientele, so, if a librarian is truly committed to the profession, he or she naturally tends to take on more and more responsibilities in an effort to be of service to more people. In fact, directors of academic, state, public, and special libraries report that one of their serious time management problems is taking on too much work at once.[8]

Librarians, as a group, need to learn that trying to please everyone often results in pleasing no one. By making commitments in an effort to accommodate everyone who asks you to do something, you may spread yourself so thin that you cannot devote the time necessary to meet any of your commitments adequately.

To combat the tendency to accept too many duties and responsibilities, one must first analyze why she may be tempted to take on more. One should never accept new responsibilities primarily to please another person. Instead, one's own personal and professional goals and objectives should be the reason.

Some professional librarians view accomplishments from a quantitative rather than a qualitative standpoint and thus readily accept new duties in the belief that the more they take on, the more they will accomplish. Instead, the good time manager concentrates on quality rather than quantity. A librarian who is already overextended should decline requests to take on more responsibilities. Learn to say no constructively.

First, be careful not to give any visual cues that indicate agreement. Many people tend to nod their heads while others are speaking as indication that they are listening actively. However, the speaker might interpret that as agreement. Nodding one's head through a conversation, then responding negatively to a request sends mixed signals to the person making the request. Instead, indicate active listening by verbal reaction.

Second, respond quickly to the request. Pondering it may raise false hopes.

Third, give reasons why you decline. It may be that the person requesting simply has no concept of how busy a librarian typically is. For example, at the beginning of a campaign for a small addition to an academic library, an architect visited the college president and the librarian. The architect explained that he needed to submit a goals and objectives statement to the agency funding the construction, with specifications for furnishings and a rough floorplan to begin the campaign. Without hesitation, the president said, "We can have that to you in a week." To which the librarian replied, "No, planning takes longer than that. First, we will need to get the opinions of library staff and consultants as to what the library's greatest needs are now and what they are likely to be in the future. Then, we will need to get specific information from library furniture manufacturers, shelving manufacturers, and a host of other vendors." This college president simply had no idea what a librarian should do to plan a building addition.

Fourth, offer alternatives. Suggest someone else who could do the job or another way the job could be accomplished. After the college librarian confronted the president about the proper way to plan a library building, the two agreed on a process that would take about six months, and the documents were ready on schedule.

Overcommitment can develop innocently, almost benignly in libraries when staff vacancies occur. A reduction in staff, either by a mandated reduction in force or by resignation or retirement, translates into increased workloads for the remaining staff, so almost inevitably some rearrangement in service or library operation must follow.

Librarians must be honest with their institutions and their clientele about the effects of staff vacancies. Advance warnings are preferable to apologies afterwards. So, give as much advance notice as appropriate to explain, for example, that interlibrary loan service might be somewhat slower than usual since the librarian responsible for that has maternity leave planned and will not return for six months.

If a permanent cutback in services is necessary due to a reduction in force, involve the library staff and your clientele in the planning process. Be open to suggestions, but also be realistic about the situation. You cannot expect your library to operate on the same level if your staffing level has dropped, and your clientele must understand that as well.

TELEPHONE TECHNIQUES

Telephone calls are at once the greatest helps and the greatest annoyances to good time management because calls to other people help get work done efficiently, but other people's calls serve to interrupt one's own work flow. Every librarian has a war story to tell about a call that came in just before quitting time and proved to be a major disruption; in fact, librarians identify telephone interruptions as one of their chief problems in managing their time effectively.[9] As a result, some librarians may actually despise the telephone for what it might bring.

However, librarians and telephones cannot be separated for long because each are part of a central purpose—communication. As the intermediaries between clientele and the knowledge that they seek, librarians must be communicators.

Despite all the frustration that it sometimes brings, the telephone remains a very effective means of communication. So, when a telephone call threatens to interrupt at the end of a busy day, librarians might do well to remember that their jobs involve communication and think to themselves, This is my job calling. That little change in attitude can go a long way toward preserving sanity.

Further, people form an opinion as to the quality of an institution at least partly from the manner in which its employees communicate by telephone. Poor telephone manners project a poor image. Although that call coming in just one minute from closing may seem like the fiftieth call in the last hour to a library staff member, it is likely to be someone calling the library for the first time that day. Answering any less enthusiastically than the first call of the day can create the wrong impression in the caller's mind.

While it sometimes may seem hopeless to fight the interruptions that a telephone may cause, in fact, librarians can manage by using the following techniques.

*1. Decide before the telephone rings whether you will
answer it.*

If you are concentrating on something important, you might choose
not to answer the phone, particularly during the time that you have
reserved to focus on your priority tasks. Generally, take the known over
the unknown. You have no idea what the telephone call concerns, so, if
you are working on a high-priority task, stay with that. If the matter is
truly important, the caller will call back.

2. Screen all telephone calls.

Obviously, this is easier in libraries that provide secretarial assistance
or receptionists to all of the professional staff. In answering the phone,
the secretary should set the expectation that you are not available. Instead
of asking, May I say who is calling? the secretary should say, She is in
a meeting. After the secretary learns the identity of the caller, she can
put appropriate calls through with an explanation such as, I know that
she will want to talk with you. This technique allows the secretary to
weed out inappropriate calls, such as those from telemarketers.

*3. Give your secretary or receptionist a permanent list of
people whose calls you will always take.*

If someone on the list calls, the secretary knows to interrupt you. If
you are an academic librarian, your list might include deans, faculty
members, the president of your institution, and other academic librarians.
If you are a public librarian, the city manager or other municipal officials,
members of the city council or board of aldermen, and, perhaps,
representatives of the press will be on your list. If you are a working
parent, the name of the director of your day-care center or the principal
of your child's school should be at or near the top of your list.

*4. Each day, give your secretary or receptionist a
temporary list of people whose calls you will take.*

The daily list will depend on the priority tasks that you have identified
for the day. For example, as you make arrangements to attend a library
conference, your travel agent might be on your daily list. After the
reservations are made, you can delete that person's name from the daily
list.

5. Use a beeper, paging system, or answering machine.

Using a beeper, paging system, or answering machine can be very effective in helping not to miss telephone calls. While paging systems would create a noise disturbance in some libraries, many so-called beepers can now operate almost completely silently.

6. Install cordless telephones at key areas.

Using cordless phones at the circulation desk, at the reference desk, and in the technical services work area will give staff members freedom of movement and reduce the number of return calls they have to make. Having a cordless phone available allows them to keep a caller on the line while checking the shelves or the catalog for an item, thus giving more direct service to the library's clientele, too.

7. Make the caller take responsibility for interruptions.

During periods when you do not want to be disturbed, the library secretary or receptionist should not ask, May I say who is calling? when answering the phone. Instead, he or she should say, She is in a meeting, Do you want me to interrupt? That forces the caller to take responsibility for evaluating his or her call and deciding whether the matter warrants an interruption. Many "important" matters become less important when the caller must take responsibility for the interruption. This technique works especially well with sales calls from publishers. Sales representatives usually do not want to risk a potential customer's wrath by interrupting her to deliver a sales pitch.

8. Schedule an appointment in the daily calendar to make telephone calls and to return them.

Place and return calls just before lunch and late in the day. You and the other person will be more likely to conduct the business of the call faster during those times. Further, scheduling a block of time on your work and appointment schedule for telephone calls insures that nothing else less pressing will take your attention.

9. Prepare an agenda for each telephone call.

Frequently, many people finish an important telephone call only to realize that they forgot to ask an important question, necessitating an immediate call back to the person with whom they were talking. To avoid that problem, librarians should treat each telephone call that they make like a meeting, albeit a long-distance meeting. To prepare for a meeting, librarians compile an agenda, so the same should be true for a telephone call. The agenda for the call can also serve as a reminder of the subject if the person called is not available. That will prevent the puzzling question when the person returns the call, Now, what was I calling about?

10. Practice good manners when calling.

At the beginning of a telephone call that you make, ask, Are you in a meeting? not, Are you busy? You can assume that most of the people whom you call are busy, but they are probably too polite to tell you so. Asking about a meeting before you launch into the business portion of the call gives the person you called a quick opportunity to handle the call at her convenience.

11. Set the expectation for brief conversations.

Set the expectation that your call will be brief by saying, This will only take a minute. Then, open the conversation with the question that you made the call to ask. If someone has called you, you can still set the expectation by saying, I have only a few minutes to talk, I have things on my schedule that I must get to. That encourages the caller to get to the point of the call.

12. Postpone discussion of health and family until the end of the phone call.

Wait until you have handled the business portion of the call before making inquiries about one's health and happiness. Of course, this technique works best with people that you do not know well. If you know the person well, you can ask politely, How are things going?, handle the business of the call, and then visit if you both still have the time.

13. Time your telephone calls.

Keep a timer by your phone and turn it over when you start talking. When the sand runs out, start winding up the conversation.

14. Sign off with verbal cues.

Develop verbal cues to end the conversation. Summarize the conversation with something like, You need a copy of this article by Wednesday for your speech to the Rotary Club on Thursday, I'll get right to it. By offering immediate action, you make it appear that the other person would be hindering your job performance if she continued talking.

15. Avoid telephone tag.

Telephone tag begins when you call someone who is not available who then returns the call when you are not available. If you get involved in a telephone tag situation, put a stop to it. Ask the person answering the telephone when would be a good time to return the call, then leave a detailed message stating when you will call again as well as a good time for you to be called.

One low-cost alternative to the telephone is electronic mail, available at most academic libraries through telecommunications networks such as BITNET. With electronic mail, a caller can leave a simple or detailed note without the fear of it being garbled at the other end by the person taking the message.

16. Shortcut telemarketing calls.

Break into the caller's presentation to explain politely, but firmly, that you do not order books, or whatever is being sold, over the phone. State that library policy prohibits telephone orders, and you cannot disregard the policy on the spur of the moment.

If the telemarketer is employed by one of your regular vendors, ask your customer service representative to note on your library's records that you do not want to receive telemarketing calls. Many vendors now keep this kind of information in a customer profile database, and they will not want to risk alienating you by continuing to call.

Further, you can notify the Telephone Preference Service of the Direct Marketing Association, 6 East 43rd St., New York, NY 10017, to request that its members be notified that you do not want telemarketing calls.

4

Time Management Techniques for Library Administrators

In addition to the techniques for better personal time management and those which involve other staff members that are described in previous chapters, librarians who supervise other librarians or support staff have additional strategies to use to improve the overall time management for the library. The strategies in this chapter are designed specifically for library administrators.

THE MISSION OF THE LIBRARY

The most effective library staff members are those who have a clear understanding of their library's mission, but many library administrators overlook the importance of developing a mission statement that sets forth clearly the goals of the library, explains the services that the library offers, and identifies the library's primary and secondary clientele. Just as librarians need to have clearly stated goals for both personal and professional development, the library must have corporate goals identified that provide direction to staff members for the services that their library provides. So, the cornerstone for effective, focused library services is a well-defined mission statement.

In addition to a proclamation of goals, a good mission statement identifies the library's clientele and describes appropriate levels of service offered to each client group. If the library serves a secondary clientele, the statement will differentiate the levels of service between the two groups.

Most library staff members have no inherent knowledge of the proper mission of a particular library. A well-drafted mission statement serves a valuable purpose because it informs the staff of the library's mission and thus provides a focus to their efforts. Obviously, the most effective staff members are those who provide high-quality services to the appropriate library users.

Once the mission statement has been adopted, library administrators should review it at least annually. Because libraries function in such a dynamic environment, changes may be necessary from time to time. Too often, though, administrators suffer from the we-don't-have-time-to-plan syndrome, or, worse, the we-don't-need-to-take-time-to-plan syndrome. In reality, most administrators can not afford *not* to take time to adopt a mission statement. Otherwise, library employees may have a mistaken view of the institution's true purpose and exert their best efforts in activities that do not support the library's mission.

MANAGEMENT STYLES

Effective time management for the library and for library staff members depends in large part on effective personnel management skills. If administrators exercise good personnel management, much less time is wasted by library employees due to confusion, conflict, or carelessness.

Good library administrators know their styles of management and whether their styles are effective with their employees. Just as library administrators differ in their styles of management, so do library staff members differ in their need for supervision. Effective personnel management, and thus effective time management, exists when the administrator's style matches the needs of her employees.

Assess your effectiveness by first recognizing your preferred style of working. Many library administrators prefer working in broad concepts, leaving to other staff members the task of filling in the details. Library administrators who work this way typically delegate tasks frequently, but they may overlook the fact that some of their employees need to have specific instructions on how to complete a particular task to feel confident in doing the job.

Other administrators like to develop an idea fully before involving other staff members. This style works well with employees who prefer detailed instruction, but some may want to be more involved with the planning process so that they can be more creative in their jobs. Further, if the project requires the establishment of particular deadlines, most staff members want to be involved since those decisions would directly affect their workloads.

In making decisions, some library administrators pride themselves on being able to decide matters quickly and move on to the next problem. These administrators respond quickly to urgent situations, but, in responding similarly to a nonurgent problem, they preclude staff members from offering valuable input.

Other administrators tend to make each decision in a more contemplative manner and involve staff at all levels before deciding. Following this style, these library administrators receive the benefit of input from staff members. However, when decisions must be made quickly or when staff members cannot receive full data needed to make a decision because of confidentiality or other concerns, these administrators become less effective than they could be.

Library administrators who remain flexible will be the most effective. If a library administrator can shift her managerial style to fit the needs of her employees or the needs of the situation, she will manage the personnel in her charge better, and, consequently, be a better time manager.

PERSONNEL SELECTION AND TRAINING

After the mission statement, a library supervisor's most important responsibility concerns the selection and training of library personnel. Hiring and training new personnel properly supports good time management by preventing problems that would take time to confront later. Traditional library school curricula exclude training in such areas as personnel selection, leaving many librarians in a quandry. While they understand the value of proper employee selection and training, they lack the rudimentary skills to do it.[1]

1. Develop procedures manuals and review them periodically to keep them current.

Procedures manuals can be important aids in training a new library employee, but their value depends on the extent to which they have been revised to reflect accurately the procedures that library employees follow. Because libraries are dynamic environments, staff members must often revise procedures to better serve the library's clientele. If the manuals are kept reasonably current, logically they should be the beginning point for staff training. However, if a procedures manual is significantly out-of-date or does not exist for a particular job, a library supervisor should wait until the new employee has been trained before beginning to assemble a new manual.

2. *Select the right person to fill a vacant position.*

Contact the references listed on an applicant's resume, and locate persons not listed who would have independent knowledge. For example, if the applicant fails to list a reference from his or her last job, investigate the situation, if you can, without violating a pledge of confidentiality. Time spent now selecting the right person for the job will save time later. Filling the position with the wrong person creates the need to spend more time than necessary in supervision and perhaps ultimately in disciplinary action.

3. *Train the new employee correctly.*

Do not rely heavily on the outgoing employee to train her replacement, and do not involve the outgoing employee in the training program at all if she had problems that resulted in disciplinary action. Even in the best of circumstances the outgoing staff member is likely to suffer a bit of "short timer's disease," looking forward to the last day at the library and what waits beyond, rather than concentrating on work. And, if she has been subject to disciplinary action, she will not be the best role model for the replacement. So, the new employee's supervisor should take a major role in developing an orientation and training program.

To fight the negative effects of compartmentalization, the lack of knowledge of overall library operations on the part of staff members, the training program for all new staff members should include an orientation to the operations of all library departments.

Some libraries require new staff members to spend half days for their first six weeks rotating through the various departments, spending one week in cataloging, one in acquisitions, and so on. While working in the other departments, the new staff member is required to learn all of the major routines and procedures.

The more time a new staff member spends in the other departments, the more she will understand the overall operation of the library. Librarians who know how their libraries operate are more effective because they know specifically which staff members to approach with problems that need attention.

4. *Include time management and values clarification in regular performance evaluations.*

Encourage employees to set goals and objectives that can be measured objectively and help develop strategies to achieve those goals. Suggest time management techniques that might make the employee more effective, and listen for suggestions on improving your effectiveness, as well.

ESTABLISHING GOALS AND PRIORITIES

The library staff members that you supervise should develop personal and professional goals, just as you should, as discussed in chapter 2. While an employee's personal goals fall outside of the responsibility of the library supervisor, the employee's professional goals and the objectives based on them should be established with the consultation and approval of the supervisor.

Further, these goals and objectives should be reviewed as part of a regular employee evaluation process. That is, regularly, the supervisor should provide the employee with a performance evaluation. The supervisor should base that evaluation, at least in part, on the extent to which the employee has made progress towards the satisfaction of her objectives and the attainment of her goals.

At least annually, each supervisor should review her employee's goals and objectives to insure that they are in harmony with her own and with the overall mission and goals of the library. These three sets of goals must not conflict with each other to insure the effectiveness of both employee and supervisor.

Similarly, the library supervisor must review each day the priority tasks identified by her employees. Employees may assign to a particular task a much higher or much lower priority than their supervisors, resulting in some unproductive work time. To be effective on a daily basis, both employee and supervisor must work according to the same general understanding of the priorities among the tasks to be completed.

Further, library supervisors should involve staff members as much as possible in establishing deadlines. If a survey, for instance, requires the collection and compilation of certain information, rather than establishing a deadline unilaterally, a good supervisor will consult the staff member to set the deadline together. That might mean shuffling the priority tasks that the staff member is currently working on, so the supervisor should be involved in making that decision.

TIME THEFT

Time theft is the deliberate waste of time by an employee, but many employees probably do not recognize it as a time management problem. Time theft includes clock watching, personal grooming, arriving late, leaving early, extending coffee breaks, placing and receiving personal telephone calls, correcting careless mistakes, extensive socializing, inattention to the job, operating a business on the side, and reading novels and other personal material on company time. Each of these habits deprives the library of the fullest and best efforts of its employees.

As a library director or supervisor of library staff members, examine carefully what you believe your library work ethic to be. Most library staff members will live up or down to the expectation and the example set and tolerated by the library director and professional staff. For example, there may be a feeling among your staff that punctuality is not important. Staff members may trickle in over the first 15 minutes or more of each morning if library management tolerates that.

As an effective time manager and supervisor, you should work to change the ethic at your library if time theft is a problem. First, avoid time theft yourself to set a good example to other library staff members. Then, seek commitment from other library employees to do the same.

PERSONAL COMMUNICATION

At times, library supervisors may confuse efficiency (doing the job right) with effectiveness (doing the right job) in communicating with staff members by writing memos rather than communicating in person. Writing memos as a means of communication can be far more efficient for a supervisor than taking the time necessary to talk personally with all of her employees when collecting information.

However, good time management concerns being effective, sometimes at the sake of efficiency. While personal communication may not be efficient, it is often more effective than dealing with staff members largely by memo. Personal communication keeps morale high, and it provides for an exchange of information not possible through written memoranda. So, err on the side of personal communication in most situations beyond mere information dissemination.

EMPLOYEE CONFLICT

The best and worst aspects of a library administrator's job involves working with people. When library employees succeed in their jobs, a library administrator experiences exhilaration and satisfaction, sharing vicariously in the employees' triumphs. But, when things go wrong, an administrator experiences the worst part of the job, strong feelings of disappointment, frustration and discouragement.

Resolving a conflict between library staff members, particularly one in which an administrator herself is involved, presents the biggest challenge to a library manager. Some conflict in libraries is inevitable because of the differences inherent in library employees. Each staff member has different interests and priorities, and each has a personal sense of motivation that may differ greatly from her coworkers. Each person working in a library is unique, and, with any collection of unique individuals, some friction will surface as staff members work toward the attainment of their professional goals and the goals of the library.

Normally, most friction between individuals can be worked out easily if both staff members are accommodating. However, conflict results when employees, for any reason, choose not to acquiesce, and, in those situations, library administrators must resolve the conflict constructively. Serious conflict between library employees cannot be tolerated because of its disabling effects on library operations.

First, determine the real problem. Ask those involved to state their perceptions of the problem, if they can do so objectively. If the participants become too emotional, wait until they regain their composure to proceed. Resolving the conflict will be far more difficult if someone becomes angry or hurt in the process. Above all else, the library administrator involved must keep her own emotions under control.

Second, use good communication skills throughout the resolution process. Summarize and restate the participants' comments to insure understanding and accuracy. Avoid being drawn into the argument by stating the comments objectively and summarizing what the participants themselves have said. Ask the participants to acknowledge the accuracy of the summary of their comments.

Proceed towards resolution of the problem when the participants and you agree on what the problem is. State the problem in terms of its negative effect on library operations. That is, differences of opinion between library employees do not become a library administrator's business until those differences cause a disruption in the operations of the library. When library work suffers, the administrator must help resolve the conflict. Stress the fact that the conflict cannot be tolerated because it disrupts the effectiveness of the library.

In seeking a solution to a conflict between library employees, the library administrator should keep in mind certain objectives. The resolution should provide a solution that is fair to both parties, establish a working relationship free of hostility, and institute channels of clear communication between the participants and library administration.

Encourage the participants themselves to determine an appropriate solution, but make suggestions to foster a sense of compromise and reconciliation. Use a comment to introduce your ideas such as, I would like to know your reactions to some suggestions that I have, and you might have your own ideas that would work better.

If necessary, suggest that another person be asked to help mediate a solution. Someone higher in library administration or from a different department may be more objective and able to suggest other solutions.

DECISION MAKING AND PROJECT PLANNING

Library supervisors face an interesting challenge in applying time management strategies in the process of decision making. Supervisors who use a participatory style of management involve many staff members under them in the decision-making process. In doing so, they can add considerably to the time required for even routine decisions.

Time management theorists, on the other hand, stress the importance of making decisions in a straightforward, efficient manner. In the business world, of course, a delay in making a decision may cause the loss of an investment opportunity. And, while the penalties for delays in the process in the library profession may not be as severe for the institution, delays could materially affect the quality of services that the library provides.

To avoid potential problems in a library, all supervisors and employees must have a clear understanding of the chain of authority for making decisions. Library organization charts and written documents that explain committee functions and powers can provide that information, and library administrators should make them available to all library employees.

In addition, many libraries, particularly publicly-funded institutions, must involve some form of governmental participation in some of the decisions that are necessary for regular operations. While sometimes library administrators might be tempted to view these procedures as a waste of time, the net effect will be time saved because problems can be identified and resolved before they become crises.

For example, a public library with a collection development policy that has been adopted through official channels is generally less subject to criticism than one with no such official policy. If someone then challenges the purchase of a particular book as being inappropriate, assuming that the purchase falls within the guidelines of the policy, the debate will concern the propriety of the policy, not the librarian's action.

This, in turn, reduces the level of emotions that might surround the incident and provide for a more direct resolution.

Worry

Another special problem for library supervisors concerns anticipating problems. It may be natural for librarians to worry somewhat about whether their clientele are satisfied with the services that they receive. Unfortunately, most librarians hear from library users only when there are problems. Very few library users make positive comments or provide compliments for good service. And, though librarians know intellectually that the "no news is good news" adage often applies to libraries, they still worry somewhat that library clientele are not satisfied.

However, the very act of worrying, particularly about something distant in time or about which one has little control, inhibits good time management. Library administrators waste time when they worry about situations too far in advance. Often, circumstances change so significantly that any plans made have to be revised anyway.

Further, in some situations, the library or the library administrator has very little control. Some things, obviously, are beyond the control of an administrator. Rather than wasting time worrying about situations over which they have no control, administrators should focus on what they can change. The prayer attributed to Reinhold Neibuhr, requesting strength to change the things one can change, acceptance for the things one cannot change, and the wisdom to know the difference, is apropos. Library administrators should work to develop the wisdom to recognize the situations that they can control and those that they cannot, particularly since they cannot plan what they cannot control.

Keep a diary for two or three months on matters that you worry about. At the end of the time, review the diary and determine whether the things that you worried about actually occurred. Chances are excellent that the most dreaded events never happened.

Project Planning

When planning a project, library administrators should establish both a beginning and ending time for library projects, with suggestions from all employees involved. Without a specified ending time, projects can drag on because employees sense no driving force toward closure.

Since much of a library's work concerns ongoing efforts to deliver services to clientele, many library projects seem to have no end. Instead, the projects establish some type of mechanism for the compilation of information and delivery of services. Consequently, for the projects that should have an established end, librarians sometimes overlook that aspect because they are accustomed to projects that initiate continuing efforts to provide services.

Crisis Time

One further point on decision making and project planning concerns adhering too strictly to rules. Most librarians, though often prejudicially cast as inflexible rule makers and rule followers, actually respond well to changing environments. When thrust into a crisis situation, these librarians tend to do what has to be done to restore homeostasis, and then work to change what must be to prevent a reoccurrence. Library administrators can promote good time management among their staff members by granting them sufficient authority to disregard some procedures and rules to respond to trying conditions.

DELEGATION

Research indicates that most academic library directors know the value of delegation theoretically but that many do not practice it fully.[2] One indication is that a significant number of those academic library managers felt that their libraries could not function without them for six months.

Directors of special libraries, however, appear to delegate more routinely. A recent survey indicates that the staff members in special libraries make most of the day-to-day decisions about their work without involving their directors.[3]

For librarians who supervise other workers, delegation can be a very effective management tool. But, to be effective, delegation must be handled properly, and, too often, busy professionals fail to take the time necessary to do that. For example, while reviewing his calendar for the coming month, a lawyer once discovered that two of his cases were scheduled for trial in two different counties for the same day. So, he asked his new secretary to have one of the matters taken off the calendar.

A few weeks later, while waiting in a courtroom for one of those trials to begin, he got a frantic call asking why he was not appearing for trial in the other case in the neighboring county. The lawyer straightened out the mess and later asked his secretary what she had done to take the second matter off the calendar. She held up a small bottle of white correction fluid and demonstrated its use. The fault in this situation belonged not with the secretary, but with the attorney who failed to delegate properly the task of rescheduling one of his trials.

Like the attorney above, many librarians, delegate by merely assigning a staff member to do something, so the results often are unacceptable. For delegation to be effective, librarians must do it correctly.

Librarians fail sometimes to delegate because they may believe too much in their own self-importance, but, at the same time, they may fear not being needed. Everyone appreciates being needed, but, if part of one's job can be delegated to another library employee, who can be considered the indispensable cog in the wheel?

Some library supervisors may hesitate to delegate to an employee who is not happy in her job, in an attempt to be sensitive to the employee. However, withholding delegation that would normally be part of that employee's workload does a disservice to the employee, to the supervisor, and to the library as a whole. The employee needs to have a realistic idea of her job responsibilities at all times. Holding something back distorts the employee's view of her job and may create impressions of you being unfair when, later, you seek to reestablish the responsibilities.

Second, withholding delegation from another staff member prevents you from being as effective a librarian as you could be. Delegation can be a very successful time management tool, and withholding it in consideration of another library employee may be a noble thing to do. However, you will be judged for career advancements, promotions, raises, tenure, and other honors, by the results that you achieve. In other words, you might pay for your nobility in terms of your career.

Third, the other employees in the library may be left with the impression that you are "playing favorites." The perception, however warranted or unwarranted, may cause problems with other employees who will then resent doing "your" work.

If you have staff members to whom you can delegate work, consider the following points to make the delegation effective.

1. What are you overpaid to do?

Identify appropriate work to be delegated by comparing your hourly wage to that of your staff members to develop a sense of what tasks should be performed by them. All professional librarians, for example, are overpaid to do routine photocopying. That task should be delegated to secretarial staff members, library clerks, or student workers.

2. Do not delegate unnecessary tasks.

Few things destroy morale faster than spending time for results that go unused or, worse, get discarded. Unless the task has continuing value to the library, it should not be done at all, much less delegated to another staff member.

3. Select the right person for the job.

The right person for the job has the right attitude and the right aptitude. Experience may count for something, but it should not be the sole criterion.

4. Train the person properly.

Staff members cannot be expected to handle tasks for which they are not trained, particularly in crisis situations. Training requires examining the whole task, from beginning to end, with the staff member, including the reasons for the process and the specific results that you expect. It also means working closely with the staff member as he or she gains familiarity with the process, then leaving the staff member alone.

5. Delegate control and authority with the task.

You must also turn over a significant measure of authority for decision making to the other person. Otherwise, you will be interrupted so frequently to make decisions that you will be tempted to take the work back. Delegating the task means that it may not be completed exactly as you would have done it, and you have to accept that reality. Good delegation includes transferring control and responsibility to the person who performs the work.

6. Establish a reporting procedure, and then monitor progress.

Set clear deadlines for the project and institute a reporting procedure so that you will be informed of progress. Then, monitor the project informally. Asking, How's it going? during break time or in another informal setting demonstrates your interest in the project and reaffirms its importance to you in a nonthreatening situation. Above all, do not wait to check on a project until just before the deadline. By then, few adjustments can be made to correct any problems. Always check shortly after the delegation and several more times until you notice that the project is well underway.

Set definite deadlines for specific delegated tasks. Do not give ASAP as a deadline, nor accept it from someone else. ASAP no longer means "as soon as possible." It means "whenever you get to it." Instead, decide on a definite deadline.

7. Give credit to the one who completes the work.

Always pass the kudos on to the staff member to whom you delegated the work. Do not accept them as your own. The employee's success reflects well on you, too. After all, you are the one who picked the employee and trained her for the job.

8. If delegation fails, resist the urge to take the work back.

Respect the employee's pride. No one wants to look like a failure before coworkers. Further, if you take the work back, the employee may develop a somewhat careless attitude. Why take the time to be sure to get the job done right if the boss will be there to step in if things go wrong?

Instead of taking back the work, counsel the employee first. It may be a lack of communication caused the problem. Then, monitor the situation without appearing to oversupervise and delegate additional parts of the job as performance improves.

On the other hand, too much delegation may take the library manager too far away from the library. To be effective, administrators must know a good bit about the daily affairs of their own libraries. They must know, for example, how often the photocopy machines break down to see the library from the user's perspective. Only then can they be effective in developing solutions to many of the real problems affecting their libraries.

To combat the effects of too much delegation, library administrators should use the technique, *management by wandering around*, which encourages administrators to take regular walks through their libraries. These regular walks serve to bring problems to the attention of the administrator, so that she knows firsthand the state of the library.

Training Middle Managers to Delegate

One might assume that the librarians in middle management positions would learn the skills of delegation from the example set by the director. If the director delegates well, the middle managers would also. However, even those library directors who apparently follow good delegation guidelines report that their employees do not delegate well.[4] It seems that being a good role model is not enough.

Librarians in higher management positions, then, should take the time to train managers under them in the process of delegation. Those managers must understand the value of good delegation both to themselves and to their library overall. The more effective each librarian and staff member is, the more effective the library operation.

Reverse Delegation

Most people think of delegation as a process that flows down the chain of command, but delegation can flow upward as well. If a staff member comes to a supervisor with a problem, that supervisor may be tempted to say something like, Let me think about it, and I'll get back to you. But, by saying that, the supervisor has accepted the staff member's delegation. The supervisor, not the staff member, now bears the responsibility to investigate the problem, formulate options, and make the decision.

Instead, when a staff member comes with a problem, the supervisor who is a good time manager will ask the staff member whether they must discuss the problem now. If not, the supervisor will set a definite time to meet and will ask the staff member to formulate some solutions in the interim. The staff member then still bears the chief responsibility for the situation, and the supervisor still provides the amount of assistance needed. Further, a staff member involved in the formulation of a solution to a problem will support the decision more fully than one in which she had no part.

BUILDING MORALE

Keeping library staff morale high contributes to good time management. Library staff members with high morale tend to take greater pride in their work, and, consequently, their work tends to have fewer errors than library staff members with low morale. Errors in work take time to diagnose and correct, so library supervisors who work to build morale, in fact, support good time management in their libraries.

Library employees may feel low morale for a number of reasons. If a staff member experiences confusion about the duties and responsibilities of the job she performs, she may feel resentment toward a supervisor for not providing better instruction, particularly if her work must be corrected often.

Another cause of low morale is improper delegation. When library administrators fail to grant the authority to make decisions concerning a task to the employee when they delegate the work that accompanies it, the staff member may feel that she is being treated essentially as little more than a servant.

The staffs of libraries of all sizes serving all types of communities and institutions contain "unsung heroes." Certainly, the technical services staff, because of its relatively low profile in most libraries, tends to go unnoticed by library users. But, even the higher profile public services staff members do not receive positive reinforcement regularly from those library users that they serve. As such, all library staff members sometimes question the value of their work, and keeping morale high under these circumstances depends in part on an administrator praising the unsung heroes in her library for the good work that they do.

Some library supervisors keep morale high among their staff members by keeping a close eye on overall operations. Those librarians employ the technique known as *management by wandering around*, the same one effective in limiting the negative effects of delegation. Management by wandering around encourages administrators to take regular walks through their libraries, and administrators can use it to keep close contacts with library staff members. This permits library administrators to provide instant reinforcement to staff members for jobs done well and instruction when needed to correct errors.

Do not overlook the successes that the library has and celebrate them appropriately. Following a library automation project, for example, consider a ceremony of some sort to officially "close" the card catalog and to credit the members of the staff that made the project work. Public recognition helps to keep morale high.

Some library staffs celebrate all sorts of occasions with parties and may actually arouse the resentment of some staff members because of pressure placed on them to bring cakes, cookies, or other "goodies." Further, numerous celebrations can become a hindrance to performing the regular business of the library.

Some administrators use a simple technique to limit the distractions that too many parties may have and, at the same time, to preserve the beneficial morale-building effects. They designate one day a month to celebrate all birthdays of staff members that will occur that month. If they encounter a month with no staff member's birthday, they hold a small celebration anyway. Then, by rotating responsibility for the refreshments, staff members feel less of an imposition.

Administrators can also help build morale by choosing to eat lunch occasionally with staff members in a library conference room or work area. Some go so far as to establish a regular program of brown-bag lunches, spending one lunch hour every two weeks with staff members. These lunches build personal relationships in an informal setting that can help with morale.

Many academic institutions provide their librarians with the option to take sabbaticals or some other type of paid study leave. These, obviously, are major perquisites of the academic world, and they provide excellent ways to restore one's energies.

ENCOURAGE TIME MANAGEMENT AMONG STAFF MEMBERS

Brainstorm at staff meetings for tips or changes that would improve library operations, and be certain to include the clerical and secretarial workers. Often, the keenest insights and suggestions for becoming more efficient and effective come from the support staff members and clerical workers.

Look for ways to simplify the work routines of all library staff members. For example, putting a cordless telephone at the reference desk might eliminate the need to make many return calls because the reference staff member could take the telephone directly to the catalog or shelf while the caller is still on the line.

Check periodically with coworkers and members of your staff for their suggestions of ways in which you could be more effective. They have an outsider's perspective and may be able to give you valuable suggestions for improving your own time management. As part of this, ask how you can support them in better time management. They might suggest, for example, that you limit interruptions more or schedule staff meetings at a different time.

Most important, though, library administrators must provide appropriate recognition to staff members whose management of time improves. Personal recognition provides strong motivation to continue to succeed.

THE PROBLEM PATRON

Beyond relations with library staff members, though, administrators should also employ good time management techniques in dealings with library users. One challenging group of library users are the so-called problem patrons.

Every library that serves a broad client base has problem patrons who want information immediately that takes days to collect and compile. They want services that the library cannot provide for any one of a number of reasons, and they behave in a rude and insulting manner.

Librarians, though, can adopt time management techniques to deal effectively with these difficult and demanding library users. The key to success, as with many other time management techniques, is proper preparation.

1. Use written library policies whenever possible.

Showing library users a written policy can deflect some of their anger because they realize that you are not acting arbitrarily to deny them service. The dynamics of the situation can shift then from personal confrontation to policy revision. Offer a brief explanation and refer them to library administration for information on changing the policy.

If you are the library director, be courteous to the disgruntled library user, but be cautious about making exceptions to the policy or changing it without proper study. In making a hurried decision, you may create many more problems that will require much more time to solve.

2. Maintain personal control.

Excuse yourself if you feel your emotions getting the best of you. Situations can spiral out of control if the participants cannot manage their emotions. Take the time first to get emotions under control, or the situation will become far more difficult to contain.

3. Offer what you can, and be honest about limitations.

Some library users are unaware that every library has certain restrictions under which it operates. Explaining the restriction and offering alternatives may help make the message easier to accept. Copyright law, for example, may prevent a public library from allowing a patron to watch the videocassette of a particular movie in a library viewing room. But, if a library also provides portable videocassette players to check out, the library user can watch the movie at home.

4. Analyze the situation afterward, then move on.

If you can learn anything from the situation, note the lesson for your use, then move on to the next project. Do not allow yourself to brood about a confrontation with a difficult library user. Brooding is a form of preoccupation that can prevent you from completing the most important tasks for the day, thus affecting your ability to manage your time well.

5

Time Management in Special Situations

Librarians can use several time management techniques for situations beyond their routine work. Preparing for the special situations discussed here by using the suggested techniques will promote increased effectiveness in one's personal and professional life.

ANNUAL REPORTS

If you are not prepared, producing an annual report can be an exercise in frustration and a real time leak. Often, librarians postpone compiling and preparing annual reports until the last possible minute, and information that could and should have been collected all year is assembled just before a deadline. Under that kind of pressure, few librarians can provide the thoughtful analysis and planning that should be the cornerstone of an annual report.

Most library annual reports contain some statistical information. In small libraries, collecting and compiling this information may be easier than in large public or academic libraries, but, if you are not prepared fully to collect and assemble the data, statistics can be a nightmare regardless of the size of your library.

Of course, library statistical reports vary greatly in their scope and depth, but an important time management point can be made despite the variety. Stay in close contact with whoever receives your library's annual report so that what you report is what is needed. Then, knowing what information you need, establish library procedures to collect and compile it efficiently.

If you have advance warning concerning a change needed in your annual report, make the necessary changes immediately to collect and compile the information requested. Doing so will prevent frustration later about having to decide whether to compile information that you have not been collecting or choosing to omit what is requested.

Another part of many annual reports concerns professional development of the librarians. Many reports require information on the librarians' professional activities for the year. So, every year, many librarians strain to reconstruct by memory alone the important and noteworthy events and accomplishments of their year for this section of the report.

Instead of relying on memory, make the job much easier by keeping a personal file labeled "Accomplishments" for each year. As things occur, drop a note into the file. If someone thanks you for service above and beyond the call of duty, place a note of it into the file. Then, when summarizing the year for the annual report, you will be far less likely to omit something important or something that could be beneficial.

TIME MANAGEMENT LUNCHES

Because librarians often have some flexibility with their lunch hours, they can use that time for a wide variety of opportunities, including some related to work or career advancement and some completely personal activities.

The "Power Lunch"

Much has been said and written both praising and criticizing the business lunch. In the library profession, business lunches remain as a device that booksellers and other vendors use to conduct some business, and this tradition will probably continue as long as salespersons and customer representatives travel.

However, one of the newer topics of discussion is the *power lunch*. The power-lunch concept concerns opportunities for building a network of professional contacts who can help with career advancement and other business matters.

Because the profession depends to a large extent on personal contacts, librarians know the value of the power lunch. Having professional contacts outside your institution enables you to serve your own clientele better since few, if any, libraries in the world are self-sufficient. Librarians must rely on other librarians for special favors, such as tricky or unusual interlibrary loans, and having extensive personal contacts can enable a librarian to be more effective at serving her clientele.

Using power lunches to develop local contacts also makes a librarian more effective. For example, an academic librarian who knows the head of the institution's department of purchasing on a first name basis can be more effective in her job. Just by placing a phone call, she can cut through the mountains of red tape that accompanies an errant purchase requisition or purchase order.

The Working Lunch

Some library directors replace the traditional staff meeting occasionally with an in-house working lunch. They find that they can review library projects in progress in a less structured atmosphere. Further, because of its more casual nature, working lunches provide an excellent opportunity for brainstorming and creative thinking among staff members.

Some library directors schedule regular brown-bag lunches with library staff members, though they set a ground rule that no one can talk about work. At first glance, it appears that these directors do not use lunch for work. But, in reality, they use lunch for the very important business purpose of building and maintaining staff morale.

The School Lunch

Some librarians might choose to use their lunch hours for learning. Often, libraries are located close to educational institutions, and one can take formal coursework. Beyond that, of course, are the programs that many public libraries offer. Even if you cannot enroll in a formal class or attend special programs, you could use your time for reading, either for pleasure or education.

The Workout Lunch

A popular choice is the noon hour workout. You may have a gym or health club available at your institution or nearby where you could exercise before having lunch. Working out just before lunch has the added benefit of keeping you peppy during the afternoon, allowing you to get much more accomplished.

The Personal Lunch

Another possibility is the volunteer lunch. You might find that you can use your lunch break to work with church and civic groups. Many busy people can find time to meet that way.

What to Eat

Despite how you use your lunch time, follow one rule: eat light. Heavy lunches, particularly those that include alcoholic beverages, bring on a sluggish feeling that will slow you down for several hours. Eating light foods such as salads and sandwiches as opposed to baked dishes will help prevent that sluggish, need-to-take-a-nap feeling.

Further, if you are eating out and are on a tight schedule, pass up dessert. Many servers in restaurants seem to slow down toward the end of a meal, so having dessert may take you longer than you expect.

TRAVEL

Good time management on a business trip begins before one leaves the library. Prepare for departure by talking with staff members about any work that you expect finished while you are gone. Also, discuss with them any special projects that you are working on so that the telephone calls and correspondence concerning these that come while you are gone will not be a surprise.

Take a look as well at your in-box before you leave. To prevent a mountain of material there when you get back, handle what you can before departing.

Reconfirm all reservations and schedules before departing. It is a simple rule, but it is often overlooked, even though it carries potentially disastrous consequences. Weather conditions, financial stability of the carrier, construction, traffic congestion, and a host of other factors can affect travel.

If you travel by air and plan to work during the flight, request a window seat. You will have fewer interruptions because flight attendants tend to dote more over the passengers seated along the aisle, and you will not be disturbed by other passengers on their way to the restrooms. Sitting in a window seat can help you discourage unwanted conversation with other passengers, too. Looking out the window deters the other people from interrupting you.

Start the trip off right by getting to the airport early. Rushing to make a flight raises your stress level, and it may take some time to get settled down enough to concentrate on work.

On the other hand, if you get to the airport too early, you face an increased risk of lost luggage. Some airlines contract with other carriers to handle the baggage of its passengers, and, if you check in too early when traveling on an airline that has contracted for baggage handling by another airline, your baggage can arrive at your destination far ahead of you. When that happens, airlines treat your luggage as unclaimed baggage and move it into storage, making retrieval more time-consuming.

Portable computers can turn travel time into work time, but you should take care when bringing a computer along on a trip, particularly if you travel out of the United States. Well in advance of your travel date, contact the customs office to discuss what arrangements may be necessary for your computer. If your library owns the computer that you plan to take, you may need to obtain an export license. Anticipate delays in processing paperwork and begin the process early.

If you plan to work during layovers, avoid the lounges. The tables generally are too small, and the atmosphere is not conducive to concentrated work. Instead, if you travel frequently enough to justify the cost, consider joining an airline club. Most provide excellent facilities for working which will allow you to concentrate up to the moment necessary to leave for your flight.

Some business travelers carry a copy of the Official Airline Guide so that, if their original flights are cancelled, they can determine quickly what their options are. The airline that cancelled the flight will make arrangements generally that are most convenient for the airline. Having an independent source of information about alternate flights sometimes pays off because you can bargain for a flight that is more convenient for you.

If your schedule at your destination is likely to be tight, avoid checking any luggage. Your luggage will not get lost, and you will not have to wait at the terminal for the baggage handlers to unload all of the other baggage. Carrying on all of your luggage will get you started faster when you arrive at your destination.

If you plan to work on your trip, take along more work than you think that you can accomplish. Unexpected delays may provide you with more time for work than you had planned, and you will be prepared to take advantage of the opportunity.

Use travel time for professional reading. Since interruptions can be minimal, you can use the time to catch up on the journal articles that you have been putting off.

You can also use travel time for long-range planning or concentrated thought about a problem. Again, because interruptions likely will be minimal, you will have an excellent opportunity for planning.

If you plan an extended trip, consider having your library ship your incoming mail to you via an overnight delivery service so that you can keep up with work at home. That way, you will not face a mountain of paperwork when you return, and your desk will be as clean as when you left.

As you begin your return, prepare a list of things to do when you are back and assign priorities to the tasks. Planning ahead for your return will help you hit the ground running and minimize your readjustment time.

If your institution requires some paperwork for reimbursement of travel expenses, keep a detailed log and prepare all expense reports and other paperwork before you return home. Trying to reconstruct a record of expenses can be difficult after you return, even if the trip is still fresh in your mind. Take one of your institution's expense report forms or prepare a custom form to help you track expenses. You will save time in submitting your reimbursement.

And, for long family trips, plan to return home at least two days before returning to work and school. You and your family need time to readjust and rest before beginning the regular routine again.

6

Balancing a Career and Personal Life

Perhaps the most challenging time management situation facing many librarians today is that of balancing the demands of a career with those of personal life. Recent studies have indicated that the amount of leisure time has actually decreased over the past decade, rather than increasing as had been predicted.[1] As a result, many people may feel the need to manage their time better to accomplish what they want at home as well as at work.

The demographics of the workplace have significantly changed in the past thirty years. In fact, the demographics of the workplace have been changing ever since the television shows of the 1950s and 1960s, such as "Leave It to Beaver" and "Father Knows Best," depicted the model American family as one in which the father worked outside the home and the mother worked as the home manager. For both men and women, the dramatic increase in the number of women working outside of the home has meant significant changes in the general patterns of personal life.

While some librarians do not have the added responsibility of parenting, many librarians function as a working parent, either as part of a two-worker family or as a single parent. No one really knows how many librarians balance career and family either as the single head of a household or as one of two working spouses. But, recent statistics indicate that 51 percent of women, 20 years or older, work outside their homes and that over 85 percent of librarians are female.[2] Other studies indicate that over 60 percent of women over 18 years are married and that nearly

53 percent of the women in the work force have children under the age of 18.[3] These figures suggest that many librarians have family commitments either as a working spouse, a working spouse with children, or as a working single head of a household.

As a result, many librarians experience significant demands for their attention at home as well as at work and, at least occasionally, encounter some difficulty balancing their time appropriately between these competing interests. However, many time management techniques for improving effectiveness at work can also improve effectiveness at home, and this chapter suggests some of those techniques that have been successful.

Most important, do not allow work matters to intrude on your personal life regularly. Many successful business executives balance their work and personal lives by setting very strict office rules for themselves. They do not bring work home at night, they do not work on the weekends, and they leave work by 5:30 or 6:00 P.M. every day. This helps keep work concerns at the office so that they can concentrate on family or personal matters when at home.

Further, setting strict rules about keeping work hours for work and home hours for family helps to prevent the tendency to procrastinate. If one thinks, I can take that home and work on it tonight, he will tend to get less work done during working hours. By establishing a personal rule that prohibits working at home, he will save work for the office and reserve his time at home for himself or his family.

PERSONAL GOALS

Too many people overlook the value of planning in their personal lives. Just as setting goals and establishing objectives helps focus one's efforts in one's professional life, planning in one's personal life can focus one's efforts on the accomplishment of one's most important aspirations outside of the library.

The planning process for one's personal life follows essentially the same steps as that for one's professional life. Begin by developing statements of personal principles that represent the kind of values that you find most important. Then, express those principles as goals. For example, if you have children and believe that providing them with a supportive, close family environment is important, state that value as a goal, such as, "Develop and maintain a close and supportive family life."

Then, from that statement, develop a set of objectives from which you can plan strategies in harmony with the overall principle. Using the goal statement on family life, for example, one might identify an objective such as, "Spend time in unplanned activity regularly with the children."

At the same time, plan goals and objectives in terms of long-range, mid-range, and immediate time frames. For long-range planning, think in terms of three years. What do you want to accomplish in your personal life within the next three years? Take the list of those things that you have identified, and develop strategies to accomplish those items.

Following this method, one might identify a personal goal to attain in three years as, "Move from apartment and buy a house." Then, developing strategies to accomplish this, one might decide to begin a savings program to raise the money required for a downpayment. Further, one might decide to seek a higher paying job to better afford house payments. That, in turn, might require additional education or skills training. All of these could be factors in the plan to buy a house within a three-year time frame.

The strategies for fulfilling the three-year plan might also influence one's mid-range and immediate goals. Mid-range goals would be those identified to attain in one year, and immediate goals would be those for the next six months. Obviously, these must support the long-range goals or the latter will rarely be attained. Accomplishing long-range goals begins by establishing and fulfilling steps towards those goals in the shorter time frames of six months and one year.

If a librarian lives alone, the goal-setting process for her personal life may not involve input from many other people. But, for those who live with other family members, to be effective, the goal-setting process must involve the other family members. Obviously, if one spouse's goals do not correlate well with the other spouse's, some problems will result.

FAMILY LIFE

Librarians who balance their professional careers with the demands of family life survive in a juggling act day by day. Like the performer who keeps dozens of plates spinning on the tops of tall poles, life can become hectic sometimes.

Other librarians may have postponed family commitments while they concentrate on careers, waiting for the "right time." This is not an effective long-term time management strategy because the right time seldom presents itself clearly. By postponing major commitments such as marriage, over a long period, one can lapse into the habit of procrastination. Subsequent postponements come easier, and the cycle becomes self-fulfilling.

Those librarians now involved in the balancing act between career and family have an important role in establishing their households as the training ground for the families of the future. The two-working-spouse family and the single-worker head of a household are quickly becoming the norm for family life in this country. So, what children and spouses see now will be what they expect from family life in the future.

If you want to build in them the expectation that every family member has a responsibility to the household, you must begin by asking your spouse and your children for assistance in running the household. Involve them in all aspects of family life: budgeting, shopping, cleaning, cooking, gardening, and all other household chores. Just as important as the time it will save you is the training that it will provide them.

At the same time, when involved in the balancing act between career and family, you must face questions about the type of life that you want for yourself and the kind of relationship that you want with your spouse and your children. Just as setting career goals can help you become the kind of library professional that you want to be, setting family and personal goals can help you build the kind of family life that you want.

Librarians can employ many time management techniques that they use to be more effective in professional life to be more effective in family life. Just as one might place a monetary value on a project for the purpose of deciding whether to proceed, one can do the same for personal time. For example, when shopping, is it worth three hours of personal time going to several stores to save $5.00? Thinking of time as an investment helps clarify its expenditure with family members.

Many mothers who work outside the home find that they must compromise on matters that once were very important to them, simply to avoid near total exhaustion or a sense of continual depression. In a very real sense, compromising is just a matter of setting new priorities. Some career women, for example, find when they begin or resume working outside the home that they must compromise on their previous standards relating to housecleaning and home-cooked meals. Where they once prided themselves on having immaculate houses and serving home-cooked meals every night, they now overlook a bit of dust and disarray, and they eat out more often.

KEEPING RELATIONSHIPS ALIVE

Working spouses must learn to live as a couple. That begins by understanding both the personal time patterns of your spouse and those of your own. Just as you should schedule your work day to exploit the times of day when you are at your best, as described in chapter 2, you should also consider your spouse's best times in scheduling important activities.

For example, if you are at your best in the evening and your spouse tends to fade after 8:00 P.M., you should avoid scheduling important discussions, such as family budgeting, in the evening. Instead, find another time when you both are closer to functioning at your best.

Understand each other's time terminology. Compare your definition with that of your spouse for each of the following terms: *in a little while, soon, later, late,* and *long time from now.* Conflicts will arise if one spouse has an extremely different concept of time than the other when he says, I'll be back in a little while. The more you understand about your spouse's concept of time and he understands about yours, the clearer your communication will be.

DAILY ROUTINE

Many working mothers find that a little bit of organization makes their daily routines much easier. If mornings tend to be somewhat hectic at your house as children prepare for school and adults prepare for work, organize the night before. Review with each family member what the day's plan for tomorrow will be.

Then, proceed with what can be done now. Discuss the clothes to wear the next day, and set them out on the dresser. Set the breakfast table and do whatever else can be done to minimize hassles in the morning. Then, put the kids to bed at a reasonable hour so that they get a good night's sleep.

In the morning, assign tasks to everyone. One spouse can cook while the other performs some other task. One of the children can pour milk, and so on. Develop a routine that demonstrates every member's importance in the running of the household.

DELEGATION

Delegation differs greatly in the context of family life than the context of work. However appealing the concept, one typically cannot fire one's spouse or children if they consistently turn in poor performances.

Some working parents do not delegate at home simply because they do not want to admit that they cannot manage all the details of both personal and professional life, so they never ask family members to help. "We hate to ask because we don't like to admit we cannot do it all, and we're afraid of appearing to be failures at our traditional roles after we've taken on the nontraditional one of a career. "[4]

Other working parents recruit children to help at home through a variety of means, including assigned chores. One variation on that is the establishment of a point system in which the parents award points for the completion of certain household jobs. Children earn points by washing dishes, mowing the lawn, washing clothes, and performing other tasks. Children can then spend the points on privileges or treats, such as watching television or going to a movie.

Family members can be a valuable aid in keeping the home running smoothly, regardless of how they are recruited. Helping at home gives children a realistic sense of what it takes to run a household, which will be of great benefit as they grow.

SHOPPING AND MEAL PLANNING

Most people balancing a career and a personal life could handle meal planning and preparation, including grocery shopping, more effectively than they do. First, far too many people fail to plan meals. Instead, they wait until returning home at the end of a hard day to decide what to prepare for the evening meal.

The more effective method is to plan menus at least a week ahead to take advantage of special offers at the grocery store. Planning menus does not require that you give up flexibility. You may decide at the end of a terrible Monday that you need a pizza night to boost your spirits. But, waiting until you get home each night to plan what you will eat for supper is not effective time management. Too often, because you are tired, you compromise on the easiest meal to fix, which, in turn, may not be the most healthy.

After planning menus for the week, compile the shopping list and prepare for the grocery store. Even though many librarians prepare library maps to save time for library clientele, few librarians prepare maps of their favorite grocery stores. And, while a few grocery stores provide maps, most do not. The store managers know that the more *time* you spend in a store the more *money* you will likely spend. So, to save your time and money, prepare maps of the grocery stores that you frequent.

Train family members to keep a running shopping list on the refrigerator door to keep track of items that they use up. The adults and older children can also note on the list those items that are close to running out. By using that list as the beginning of a full shopping list, the family member doing the shopping does not have to take time to survey condiments, spices, and other essentials before shopping trips.

At the store, buying in bulk quantities for items that you use frequently can reduce the number of shopping trips that you take each week. For example, if your children thrive on peanut butter sandwiches, buy peanut butter in the largest size so that you will always have some handy. However, exercise some caution so that you select only those items that you frequently use. Otherwise, buying large quantities can waste both time and money if the food spoils before it can be eaten.

Cook ahead just as you plan ahead. Cook several main dishes over the weekend and freeze them. Then, move each dinner to the refrigerator the night before you plan to eat it. Reheating something already cooked usually takes far less time than preparing and cooking it.

HOUSEHOLD RECORD KEEPING AND ORGANIZATION

Organize your household paperwork. Despite our phenomenal professional ability to create and store records at work, we sometimes fail to keep good records at home. Keep a notebook with sections labeled: to buy, to fix, to do, and to call. Running errands will become easier because all of the pertinent information is recorded.

Keep public and school library books on a special shelf in the house. That will keep them separated from the others so that they can be located quickly and easily.

AVOID TIME WASTERS

Avoid obvious time leaks like watching television too much. While the television-viewing habits of American librarians have not been studied extensively, the viewing habits of the general public raise some serious questions about the ability of people to spend their leisure time constructively.

While general surveys of opinion indicate a decrease in the amount of leisure time over the past several decades, specific demographic studies indicate a different finding. In fact, according to several detailed studies, leisure time has actually increased since 1965.[5] However, passive leisure activities, such as television watching, have increased, so most people do not realize much, if any, increase. For each additional hour of free time that Americans have gained since 1965, they spend an extra hour watching television.[6]

Instead of turning on the television immediately when you get home, try music instead so that you can work at the same time. If you have favorite programs, use a videocassette recorder to tape them so that you can watch them at your convenience, rather than changing your schedule to match that of the broadcast networks.

AVOID OVERCOMMITMENT

Limit your outside activities so that you do not spread yourself too thin. Choose only those that are most important to you. The "Supermom" myth has largely faded now, and the reality is that librarians with family responsibilities do not have time for everything.

Contract out for the activities that you have neither the interest nor the ability to do. If you have never had a green thumb and hate yardwork and gardening, hire the neighborhood teenagers to do those tasks for you.

If you like to entertain, consider hiring caterers or friends to help. Schedule two parties for consecutive nights. Unless your parties are wild affairs, your house will be relatively clean from the first party, and you can use the same theme and decorations.

Above all else, budget time for yourself. A popular bath oil advertisement uses the slogan, "Take me away!", and the advice is sound. Everyone needs some personal time, even busy librarians. They should not have to apologize for taking the vacations that everyone else does.

Perhaps what librarians need most in avoiding overcommitment is training in how to be assertive while being polite. For example, an academic librarian recently received a nonurgent request for information from a faculty member late on the day before a holiday weekend. Early on the first day after the weekend the faculty member called to see if she had done anything with the request over the weekend. She explained that she took a three-day weekend just like everyone else at the institution and assured the faculty member that she would complete the request that day. By stressing the fact that she had personal needs in a positive, nonthreatening way, she may have changed that faculty member's appreciation of librarians a little bit.

If you find the balancing act too difficult, consider making an alteration. Hiring a maid or housekeeper, even on a part-time basis, can bring needed assistance with domestic responsibilities. At work, investigate the possibility of a part-time position. Some institutions have enough flexibility in personnel administration to make that adjustment.

WEEKENDS WITH FAMILY

Since weekends constitute about one-third of one's life, they provide an important opportunity to build family relationships and to strengthen the family as a whole. However, with the hustle and bustle of the regular work week, many families overlook weekends as occasions for the application of time management principles.

Instead, working parents should use the same kind of time management processes for weekends that they do for the rest of the week. First, weekends must be planned to a much higher degree than many families often do. Rather than planning activities that would support the attainment of personal and family goals and objectives, too often, families save all errands, household cleaning, and other chores for the weekend. As a result, weekends do not provide the refreshment and revitalization that they should.

A good weekend begins with a good week at work and home. Maintain strict personal rules prohibiting library work at home to give more time during the week for household duties. Work a little each day at cleaning, laundry, or other necessary household jobs. Then, the weekend will not be devoted solely to cleaning and other routine tasks.

Second, plan the weekend's activities carefully. Provide a balance between the adults and children. Children's activities often predominate, so the adults have little opportunity to enhance their relationships. For example, a family's weekend should be organized for some activities planned primarily for the children and some for the parents. Parents should invest time each weekend to enhance their relationship.

Further, include some new activity one weekend each month. Often, people tend to overlook some of the best features of their local areas. For example, make plans to visit that museum that your family has always talked about seeing, or plan an outing to the state park nearby. Exploring new places, particularly in the local area, can provide a nice break in your family's routine.

Even with the best planning in the world, though, families must maintain flexibility. A sudden thunderstorm can dampen enthusiasm for outdoor activities and force cancellation of eagerly awaited adventures. Be prepared to switch gears, if need be, on short notice.

7

Implementing a Time
Management Plan

Implementing a time management plan for both one's personal and professional life involves several steps. First, one must identify and develop a set of goals and objectives. Second, one must combine those goals and objectives with a program of time management behaviors designed to limit the waste of time. Third, on a regular basis, one must evaluate and revise the goals and objectives as well as the time management strategies used.

This chapter includes information on how to develop and implement a program of time management using the information and strategies described in the previous chapters. In getting started, one might use the forms in the appendixes and consult some of the resources listed in the annotated bibliography, as well.

SETTING GOALS

The first step in any effective time management program involves identifying personal and professional values and establishing goals and objectives in support of those values, as described in chapter 2.

Begin by stating the personal values, or unifying principles, that you have or that you want to guide your life. If you have trouble stating these, consult some of the books and other sources listed in the bibliography that provide particular guidance in this area. Often, these resources provide sets of forms that will give some suggestions on how to get started.

One time management theorist suggests six aspects of life from which to draw one's true personal values. He describes these as six "yous": workplace you, involved with career and retirement; intellectual you, concerned with self-development; physical you, requiring exercise and proper diet; family you, involved with special activities with spouse and children; social you, concerned with pressures and opportunities from friends; and spiritual you, concerned with the religious and meditative aspects.[1] Using this framework may help you to get started identifying your own values.

There is no correct or incorrect number of personal values to have, but a list of only one principle, such as "Be happy," is too brief and overbroad. A list of 50 or more may contain a number of closely related or duplicate principles.

After listing the unifying principles, move to the next level, and identify long-term goals that support those principles. Include goals related to your professional and personal life. Then, establish objectives that will help you attain the goals that you have set.

Include as part of your time management plan a list of three major accomplishments that you want to achieve in the next month, year, and three-year period for all goals that you established for your professional and personal life. Then, create an action plan to satisfy these objectives.

Commit your time management plan—your goals, objectives, and action plan—to writing and review it at least every month. Put a reminder in your appointment calendar for the first day of each month. Some time management experts recommend keeping one's goals in plain sight throughout the day because these should be the basis for determining what the daily priorities will be.

INVESTIGATE THE REGULAR ROUTINE

After you have made your general plan of action, then examine your work habits to identify which specific behaviors you have that waste time and which good time management behaviors that you do not use. Analyze your strengths and weaknesses by recording your use of time over a fairly typical two-week period. Avoid weeks of seasonal or unusual activities.

Use the time management log sheets printed in the appendixes to document your activities, take the pages for two weeks from an old, unused appointment book, or make a log of your own design to keep as a record. To make your own, construct a chart, similar to those in the appendixes, divided by days at the top and 15-minute periods down the side.

If you use a microcomputer regularly in your work, you could also use an inexpensive time and billing system to keep track of your day. The program need not be expensive. Many suitable programs are in popular shareware collections or in the public domain.

Record the time you spend throughout the day. Be faithful and honest, and record the time as you spend it for greater accuracy. The more complete and accurate it is, the better it will help you. Develop your own shorthand so that entries are concise and easy to log in. In Figure 7.1, for example, a capital *T* means telephone call, the lowercase *o* for an outgoing call, and the lowercase *i* for an incoming call.

Figure 7.1
Time Management Log

	MONDAY	TUESDAY	WED
8:00 - 8:15	Planning for week	Revise daily plan	
8:15 - 8:30	Budget request	T-i; Ref. request	
8:30 - 8:45	" "	Mail	
8:45 - 9:00	T-i; Budget req.	T-o (2)	
9:00 - 9:15	Budget request	Reference Shift	
9:15 - 9:30	" "	" "	
9:30 - 9:45	Staff Meeting	" "	
9:45 - 10:00	" "	" "	
10:00 - 10:15	Reference Shift	" "	
10:15 - 10:30	" "	" "	
10:30 - 10:45	" "	" "	
10:45 - 11:00	" "	" "	
11:00 - 11:15	" "	Automation Project	
11:15 - 11:30	" "	" "	
11:30 - 11:45	T-o (2)	" "	
11:45 - 12:00	T-o	Workout at gym	
12:00 - 12:15	Lunch	Workout at gym	
12:15 - 12:30	"	Workout; Lunch	

After two weeks, analyze the time management practices on the log sheets, both good and bad. For example, a librarian practicing good time management will have "Planning daily schedule" recorded at the beginning of each day or at the end of the previous day. Analyze your work patterns in light of the techniques presented in the previous chapters and take steps to integrate more effective time management strategies.

CLEAR YOUR DESK

As you begin your program of time management, clear your desk completely and put everything into a box. Then, as you work through the items in the box, ask, Why do I need this, and Where will it go? If you cannot answer the first question, toss the item immediately into the trash. If you cannot answer the second question, consider whether you really need it. If you needed it again and did not have it in any library file, how much trouble would it be to replace? Unless the answer is more than a minor inconvenience, toss the item into the trash.

Be ruthless. The purpose here is to rid your most important work surface of clutter and distracting paperwork. The more you save from the box, the more time you will take dealing with it later.

READ MORE LITERATURE

If you want to read more about time management, you can consult a wealth of material in professional and trade literature. Many resources that are listed in the annotated bibliography here are readily available at local public and academic libraries.

FEEDBACK

Discuss your time management program with your supervisor and coworkers to enlist their aid. Studies have shown that the most effective method of utilizing time management techniques includes receiving reactions and suggestions for improvement from fellow workers. Therefore, seek comments and suggestions from other library staff members.

One week after beginning your program, ask fellow library staff members to list your best and your worst time management habits that they have seen. Take the bad with the good, and develop strategies for improvement. Make a similar survey one week later and then a month after that. From then on, make semiannual checks to see that you still practice good time management.

STAFF-WIDE TRAINING IN TIME MANAGEMENT

Consider establishing a staff-wide training program in time management. If all of the members of a library staff practiced good time management, the entire library would run smoother and become more productive. Therefore, library directors and those who supervise library staff members should encourage a program of time management for all staff members.

A staff-wide training program in time management has several advantages to training staff members individually. First, the training will be standard and uniform. Every staff member will hear the same message, in the same way. This helps build a sense of camaraderie which can help overcome the anxiety of learning new work routines and procedures.

Second, a staff-wide training program promotes more opportunities for creative thinking about improving overall library procedures and operations. Two staff members working together through a time management program, for example, may share thoughts that could lead to a revision in the procedures of one department resulting in significant time savings.

Third, involving all staff members in training clearly demonstrates the importance of the functions performed by support staff members to the overall operation of the library. The support staff members have a unique perspective on operations that professional librarians should not overlook, and involving all staff members gives each group an opportunity to learn from the other.

Nonetheless, any change, however small, in a staff member's work routine can be threatening. When introducing a program of time management for library staff, administrators must be prepared for resistance. Comments such as, But we've always done it this way, and That won't work here, that arise when introducing any new project in a library can also occur as the staff begins a program in time management.

To build a supportive climate, the library administration responsible for the program should communicate with staff members early on to insure complete cooperation. Above all else, library administrators should stress the purpose of the training program: to reduce staff members' workloads in order improve everyone's effectiveness.

The explanation of the program should include several other factors. First, staff members should understand that the administrators view the program as very important to the overall successful operation of the library and that full cooperation and participation is expected. If staff members regard good time management as important to them as well as to the library overall, they will more readily take part in the program.

Further, library staff members must know that appropriate changes will be made as a result of training. That is, they should feel confident that library administrators will follow training with surveys to insure that the lessons learned in the program are put to work. Likewise, staff members should be given a significant opportunity to suggest changes in their individual work routines as well as to library operations overall. If staff members know that their suggestions and opinions will be considered seriously and respectfully, they will participate more fully in the training program.

Logistics of Establishing a Staff-Wide Program

First, determine the problems that need to be addressed. To take full advantage of time management training as an individual, one would begin by surveying one's own work habits to discover areas that could be improved by the use of recognized strategies. In the same way, to receive the full advantage of time management training, the library staff collectively must study its operations. Thus, the first step in any program is to determine the time management problems in the library as perceived by staff members.

One easy way to get the staff's perception of time management problems is a survey. Prepare a list of situations including the major topics presented in the previous chapters, such as interruptions, the telephone, visitors without appointments, reference questions, and meetings. Do not leave out highly personal time management problems such as procrastination, personal telephone calls, and other problems of time theft. Ask staff members to identify the time management problems that they face individually, and also ask for an assessment of library-wide problems.

Second, after staff members have identified the problem areas, arrange for training, either from an in-house library staff member or from an outside expert. Several training companies now offer one-day seminars in time management, and institutions can contract for these programs on an individual basis. Costs vary widely, depending on the number of staff members to be trained, travel expenses, and other items.

Each approach, in-house trainer or outside speaker, has certain advantages and disadvantages. An in-house trainer can design the presentation to heavily stress those topics identified by staff members as particular time management problems. While an outside speaker should be given this same information, he may be less able or less willing to adapt his presentation.

In some situations, though, an outside speaker will bring a sense of authority and credibility that an in-house trainer will not have. In most situations, the outside speaker would be one who has studied time management extensively and led many training sessions. The in-house trainer would generally not have this experience.

Third, determine a strategy for providing feedback. After staff members have heard the presentation on the principles of time management, they should give and receive feedback on the effectiveness of their time management practices and those of other library staff members.

Schedule weekly meetings for the first month following the presentation, one meeting for two months after the presentation, and one for six months after the presentation. At these meetings, staff members should be expected to share their successes and failures in time management and to provide constructive suggestions to fellow staff members.

Following the completion of the program, consider including time management in annual employee evaluations.

OTHER TRAINING OPTIONS

A number of one-day seminar companies now include time management among their course offerings. Most of these seminars are geared to private industry, so the information provided might not work without adaption for library staff members in a publicly funded institution. However, many of the principles of good time management remain the same, regardless of the institution. These courses generally provide good quality instruction at a reasonable price.

Some staff members may prefer independent learning, and some self-paced instructional materials are available on time management, including one course designed specifically for library staff. Andrew Berner's *Time Management in the Small Library*, published by the Special Libraries Association, covers techniques for planning, fighting procrastination, and improving delegation, as well as for other topics.[2]

VALUE OF TIME MANAGEMENT

Whether one chooses to learn time management techniques through independent study of resources, a program offered by an outside company, or an in-house staff-wide training program, a librarian will recognize the value of practicing good time management even by employing just a few of the strategies learned. Good time management allows librarians to accomplish more in their personal and professional lives, and, further, to accomplish what is most important to them. As a result, librarians who practice good time management have a sense of greater self-esteem and greater career satisfaction than others who fail to realize the best use of their time.

What is the best use of your time right now?

Appendixes

SETTING PERSONAL AND PROFESSIONAL GOALS

I. GOALS FOR THREE YEARS

Within the next three years, I plan to accomplish the following in my personal life:

A.

B.

C.

Within the next three years, I plan to accomplish the following in my career:

A.

B.

C.

II. GOALS FOR ONE YEAR

Within the next year, I plan to accomplish the following in my personal life:

A.

B.

C.

Within the next year, I plan to accomplish the following in my career:

A.

B.

C.

III. GOALS FOR SIX MONTHS

Within the next six months, I plan to accomplish the following in my personal life:

A.

B.

C.

Within the next six months, I plan to accomplish the following in my career:

A.

B.

C.

TIME MANAGEMENT LOG—MORNINGS

	MONDAY	TUESDAY	WEDNESDAY	THURSDAY	FRIDAY
8:00 – 8:15					
8:15 – 8:30					
8:30 – 8:45					
8:45 – 9:00					
9:00 – 9:15					
9:15 – 9:30					
9:30 – 9:45					
9:45 – 10:00					
10:00 – 10:15					
10:15 – 10:30					
10:30 – 10:45					
10:45 – 11:00					
11:00 – 11:15					
11:15 – 11:30					
11:30 – 11:45					
11:45 – 12:00					
12:00 – 12:15					
12:15 – 12:30					

TIME MANAGEMENT LOG—AFTERNOONS

	MONDAY	TUESDAY	WEDNESDAY	THURSDAY	FRIDAY
12:30 – 12:45					
12:45 – 1:00					
1:00 – 1:15					
1:15 – 1:30					
1:30 – 1:45					
1:45 – 2:00					
2:00 – 2:15					
2:15 – 2:30					
2:30 – 2:45					
2:45 – 3:00					
3:00 – 3:15					
3:15 – 3:30					
3:30 – 3:45					
3:45 – 4:00					
4:00 – 4:15					
4:15 – 4:30					
4:30 – 4:45					
4:45 – 5:00					

Notes

CHAPTER 1. THE TRUTH ABOUT TIME MANAGEMENT

1. Helen M. Gothberg, "Time Management in Special Libraries," *Special Libraries* 82 (Spring 1991): 123–25.

2. Nancy Gibbs, "How America Has Run Out of Time," *Time* 135 (April 24, 1990): 58–67.

3. "All Work, Little Play Typical for Business People in 1988," press release for Priority Management Systems, Inc., available from S & S Public Relations, Inc., 40 Skokie Blvd., Northbrook, IL 60062.

4. Gibbs, "America Has Run Out," 58.

5. U.S. Bureau of the Census, *Statistical Abstract of the United States, 1989* (Washington, D.C., 1989), 754.

6. Janice Kaplan, "How to Beat the Clock," *Vogue* 178 (August 1988): 314.

7. Richard I. Winwood and Hyrum W. Smith, *Excellence Through Time Management* (Salt Lake City, Utah: Franklin Institute, Inc., 1985).

8. R. Franklin Gillis, Jr., *It's about Time: Time Management for Church Professionals* (Lima, Ohio: C.S.S. Publishing Co., 1989); Helen L. Collins, "When Your Job is Just One of Your Worries," *RN* 50 (August 1987):60–62; Lisa A. Flaherty, "The Results of Effective Time Management in Law Firms: Increased Productivity and Quality," *Virginia Bar Association Journal* 12 (Summer 1986):12–16.

9. Joy Berry, *Every Kid's Guide to Using Time Wisely* (Chicago: Children's Press, 1987); Joy Wilt, *A Kid's Guide to Managing Time* (Waco, Tex.: Word, 1979).

10. W. Keith Schilit and Howard M. Schilit, "Improving Your Time Management Skills," *Journal of Accountancy* 162 (July 1986): 116–21.

11. Anastasia Toufexis, "The Times of Your Life," *Time* 133 (June 5, 1989): 66–67.

12. C. Jay Slaybaugh, "Pareto's Law and Modern Management," *Management Services* 4 (March-April 1967): 53–59.

13. Richard L. Trueswell, "Some Behavorial [sic] Patterns of Library Users: The 80/20 Rule," *Wilson Library Bulletin* 43 (January 1969): 458–61.

14. Philip Marvin, *Executive Time Management* (New York: AMACOM, 1980), 3.

15. P. A. Thomas and Valerie A. Ward, *Where the Time Goes* (London: Aslib, 1973), 39.

16. Ronald G. Leach, "Finding Time You Never Knew You Had," *Journal of Academic Librarianship* 6 (March 1980): 4–8.

17. Thomas and Ward, *Where the Time Goes*, 38.

18. A. Thomas Hollingsworth and Joseph Mosca, "Managing Your Time," *Management Solutions* 33 (December 1988): 18–19.

19. Alan Lakein, *How to Get Control of Your Time and Your Life* (New York: New American Library, 1973), 30–34.

20. Charles R. Hobbs, *Time Power* (New York: Harper & Row, 1987).

21. Abraham H. Maslow, *Motivation and Personality* (New York: Harper, 1954).

22. Anita Woolfolk and Robert Woolfolk, "Time Management—An Experimental Investigation," *Journal of School Psychology* 24 (Fall 1986): 267–75.

CHAPTER 2. PERSONAL TIME MANAGEMENT TECHNIQUES

1. Henry David Thoreau, *Walden* (Roslyn, N.Y.: Walter J. Black, Inc., 1942), 51.

2. Richard I. Winwood and Hyrum W. Smith, *Excellence Through Time Management* (Salt Lake City, Utah: Franklin Institute, Inc., 1985), 28–49.

3. Daniel Stamp, "Total Priority Management," *Management Solutions* 33 (October 1988): 32–34.

4. Charles R. Hobbs, *Time Power* (New York: Harper & Row, 1987).

5. Alan Lakein, *How to Get Control of Your Time and Your Life* (New York: New American Library, 1973), 66.

6. Jim Davidson, *Effective Time Management: A Practical Workbook* (New York: Human Science Press, 1978).

7. Winwood and Smith, *Excellence Through Time Management*, 30.

8. Andrew Berner, *Time Management in the Small Library* (Washington, D.C.: Special Libraries Association, 1988), 81.

9. Jimmy Calano and Jeff Salzman, "How to Get More Done in a Day," *Working Woman* 13 (April 1988): 99–100.

10. Helen M. Gothberg, "Time Management in Special Libraries," *Special Libraries* 82 (Spring 1991): 124–25.

11. Registered trademark of Day-Timers, Inc., One Day-Timer Plaza, Allentown, PA 18195-1551.

12. Registered trademark of Quo Vadis Publications, Inc., 120 Elmview Ave., Hamburg, NY 14075-3770.

13. Registered trademark of Good Software Corp., 13601 Preston Rd., Suite 500W, Dallas, TX 75240.

14. Registered trademark of IBM Corp., P.O. Box 1328-W, Boca Raton, FL 33429-1328.

15. Registered trademark of Chronologic Corp., 515 N. Oracle, No. 210, Tucson, AZ 85704.

16. Registered trademark of Campbell Services, Inc., 21700 Northwestern Highway, Suite 1070, Southfield, MI 48075.

17. Registered trademark of Polaris Software, 613 West Valley Pkwy., Suite 323, Escondido, CA 92025.

18. Registered trademark of Primetime Software, Inc., P.O. Box 27967, Santa Ana, CA 92799-7967.

19. Registered trademark of Borland International, Inc., 1800 Green Hills Road, P.O. Box 660001, Scotts Valley, CA 95066-0001.

20. Registered trademark of Chronos Software, Inc., 555 De Haro St., Suit 240, San Francisco, CA 94107.

21. Lakein, *How to Get Control*, 96–99.

22. Robert W. Braid, "Effective Use of Time," *Supervisory Management* 28 (July 1983): 9–14.

23. Dana C. Rooks, *Motivating Today's Library Staff: A Management Guide* (Phoenix, Ariz.: Oryx Press, 1988).

24. Joseph Becker, "Libraries, Society, and Technological Change," *Library Trends* 27 (Winter 1979): 409–16.

25. Charles Osgood, "The Osgood File," Copyright ©1990 by CBS, Inc. All rights reserved. Originally broadcast on May 23, 1990 over the CBS Radio Network.

26. Registered trademark of Software Publishing Corp., 1901 Landings Dr., Mountain View, CA 94043.

27. Registered trademark of Symantec, 10210 Torre Ave., Cupertino, CA 95014-2132.

28. Registered trademark of ButtonWare, P.O. Box 96058, Bellevue, WA 98009-4469.

29. Registered trademark of AskSam Systems, P.O. Box 1428, Perry, FL 32347.

30. Registered trademark of Valor Software, 2005 Hamilton Ave., San Jose, CA 95125.

31. Registered trademark of Lotus Development Corp., 55 Cambridge Pkwy., Cambridge, MA 02142.

32. Registered trademark of Micro Logic Corp., P.O. Box 70, Hackensack, NJ 07602.

33. Registered trademark of Zylab Corp., 3105-T N. Wilke Rd., Arlington Heights, IL 60004.

34. Berner, *Time Management*, 55.

35. Vernon E. Buck, *Working Under Pressure* (London: Granada Publishing Ltd., 1972), 178.

36. Charles Curran, "Qualifications: MLS, Plus Sense of Humor," *American Libraries* 20 (May 1989): 471.

37. Nathan M. Smith, Howard C. Bybee, and Martin H. Raish, "Burnout and the Library Administrator: Carrier or Cure," *Journal of Library Administration* 9, no. 2 (1988): 13–21.

38. Ibid., 14.

39. Veneese C. Nelson, "Burnout: A Reality for Law Libraries," *Law Library Journal* 79 (Spring 1987): 267–75.

40. Gothberg, "Time Management," 124.

41. Anne Woodsworth, "Getting Off the Library Merry-Go-Round: McAnally and Downs Revisited," *Library Journal* 114 (May 1, 1989): 35–38.

42. Michael J. Slinger, "The Career Paths and Education of Current Academic Law Library Directors," *Law Library Journal* 80 (Spring 1988): 217–39.

CHAPTER 3. TIME MANAGEMENT TECHNIQUES INVOLVING OTHERS

1. Helen M. Gothberg, "Time Management in Special Libraries," *Special Libraries* 82 (Spring 1991): 123–24.

2. "8 Minutes' Worth of Work", *U.S. News & World Report* 106 (May 22, 1989): 81.

3. F. Trowbridge vom Baur, "What a Librarian can do for a Law Firm," *Practical Lawyer* 26 (January 15, 1980): 83–87.

4. Gothberg, "Time Management," 124.

5. Robert E. Brundin, "The Place of the Practicum in Teaching Reference Interview Techniques," *Reference Librarian*, no. 25/26 (1989): 449–64.

6. Marilyn D. White, "Different Approaches to the Reference Interview," *Reference Librarian*, no. 25/26 (1989): 631–46.

7. Helen M. Gothberg and Donald E. Riggs, *Time Management Study in Academic Libraries, Final Report* (ERIC Doc.267 802) (Washington, D.C.: Council on Library Resources, 1986): 49.

8. Gothberg, "Time Management," 124–25.

9. Ibid., 123.

CHAPTER 4. TIME MANAGEMENT TECHNIQUES FOR LIBRARY ADMINISTRATORS

1. Janis L. Johnston, "Training New Law Library Personnel: The Neglected, Essential Activity," *Law Library Journal* 83 (Winter 1991): 61.

2. Helen M. Gothberg and Donald E. Riggs, "Time Management in Academic Libraries," *College & Research Libraries* 49 (March 1988): 131–40.

3. Helen M. Gothberg, "Time Management in Special Libraries," *Special Libraries* 82 (Spring 1991): 121–22.

4. Ibid., 122.

CHAPTER 6. BALANCING A CAREER AND PERSONAL LIFE

1. Nancy Gibbs, "How America Has Run Out of Time," *Time* 135 (April 24, 1990): 58–67.

2. Barbara Laynor, "Librarianship and Motherhood: A Part-Time Solution," *Medical Reference Services Quarterly* 64 (Winter 1987): 15–25.

3. U.S. Bureau of the Census, *Statistical Abstract of the United States, 1989* (Washington D.C., 1989), 42, 386.

4. Diana Silcox and Mary Ellen Moore, *Woman Time: Personal Time Management for Women Only* (New York: Wyden Books, 1980), 118.

5. Blayne Cutler, "Where Does the Free Time Go?" *American Demographics* 12, no. 11 (November 1990): 36–38.

6. John P. Robinson, "The Leisure Pie," *American Demographics* 12, no. 11, (November 1990): 39.

CHAPTER 7. IMPLEMENTING A TIME MANAGEMENT PLAN

1. Daniel Stamp, "Total Priority Management," *Management Solutions* 33 (October 1988): 32–34.

2. Andrew Berner, *Time Management in the Small Library* (Washington, D.C.: Special Libraries Association, 1988).

Annotated Bibliography of Selected Resources

BOOKS

Anderson, Richard C., and L. R. Dobyns. *Time: The Irretrievable Asset*. Los Gatos, Calif.: Correlan Publications, 1973.

> Simplified approach with no background or details. Delegation, priorities, effective meetings. 67 pages.

Berner, Andrew. *Time Management in the Small Library*. Washington, D.C.: Special Libraries Association, 1988.

> Self-study program covering planning, delegation, procrastination, prioritizing, and setting deadlines. 102 pages.

Brewer, Kristine C. *Getting Things Done: An Achiever's Guide to Time Management*. Shawnee Mission, Kans.: National Press Publications, Inc., 1988.

> Handling meetings, telephone calls, stress and procrastination. Tips for women include establishing priorities at home, organizing family for meal preparation. 38 pages.

Creth, Sheila. *Conducting Effective Meetings and Other Time Management Techniques*. Chicago: Association of College and Research Libraries, 1982.

> Workbook for evaluating how time is spent, for setting goals, as well as for holding meetings. 20 pages.

Culp, Stephanie. *Conquering the Paper Pile-up*. Cincinnati: Writer's Digest Books, 1990.

> Suggestions for organizing over 100 sources of household and business information, calendars, bank statements, magazines, and political information. Many topics also appear in Culp's *How to Conquer Clutter*. 160 pages.

_____. *How to Conquer Clutter*. Cincinnati: Writer's Digest Books, 1989.

Suggestions for organizing over 100 common household and business items and types of information, including batteries, boxes, business cards, exercise equipment, photographs, souvenirs, spices, and wine. Includes "Resource Helpline" with addresses of businesses providing storage services and products. Many topics also appear in Culp's *Conquering the Paper Pile-up*. 164 pages.

Douglass, Merrill E., and Donna N. Douglass. *Manage Your Time, Manage Your Work, Manage Yourself*. New York: AMACOM, 1980.

Thorough treatment of major topics. Chapters on stress, personal performance, travel time. Summary list of 20 steps to better time management. 278 pages.

Eisenberg, Ronni, and Kate Kelly. *Organize Yourself!* New York: Macmillan, 1986.

Practical tips for personal and family organization, including time management. Subdivisions include getting control of your time, paperwork, financial records, household matters, main events, personal agenda, children. 273 pages.

Eyre, Richard, and Linda Eyre. *Lifebalance*. New York: Ballantine Books, 1987.

Time management from the perspective of balancing goals, attitudes, and priorities. 280 pages.

Gothberg, Helen M., and Donald E. Riggs. *Time Management Study in Academic Libraries, Final Report*. Washington, D.C.: Council on Library Resources, 1986.

ERIC Document 267 802. Final report of research described in the authors' *College and Research Libraries* article.

Hall, Sandy. "How Superhumans Manage Time." In *Library Management in Review*, edited by Alice Bruemmer. New York: Special Libraries Association, 1981.

List of 20 tips on managing time. 2 pages.

Hibbard, Janet G. "Who Controls Your Time?" In *Library Management in Review*, edited by Alice Bruemmer. New York: Special Libraries Association, 1981.

Planning, setting goals, organizing a work schedule and appointment book. 6 pages.

Hobbs, Charles R. *Time Power*. New York: Harper & Row, 1987.

Values-based approach to time management. Start with analysis of the kind of person you want to be, state goals, develop action plan to meet goals, then organize activities around the plan. 209 pages.

Kaufman, Phyllis C., and Arnold Corrigan. *How to Use Your Time Wisely*. Stamford, Conn.: Longmeadow Press, 1987.

GOLD principle: setting *G*oals, *O*rganizing priorities, *L*isting things to do each day, and *D*o it now! Major topics include filing and handling paperwork, interruptions, fighting procrastination, and organizing work and living space. 101 pages.

Lakein, Alan. *How to Get Control of Your Time and Your Life*. New York: New American Library, 1973.

One of the most-cited works in time management. Some information on setting goals, but very good with specific behaviors for planning each day, discouraging interruptions, handling delegation, and other techniques. 160 pages.

Lee, John W., with Milton Pierce. *Hour Power*. Homewood, Ill.: Dow Jones-Irwin, 1980.

Values-based approach stressing "why" over "how". 4 D's for handling material: drop it, delay it, delegate it, do it. Delay can be positive or negative. Positive delay includes waiting to get emotions under control before acting. 212 pages.

Mackenzie, Alec. *Time for Success: A Goal-Getter's Strategy*. New York: McGraw-Hill, 1989.

Goal-setting and time management problems (time barriers) divided into categories: human, managerial, and environmental. Planning, crisis management, and effective listening. 181 pages.

Mayer, Jeffrey J. *If You Haven't Got the Time to Do It Right, When Will You Find the Time to Do It Over?* New York: Simon & Schuster, 1990.

Topics include the importance of committing information to writing instead of relying on memory, reading to save time, and using appointment calendars and diaries. 159 pages.

Noble, Valerie. *A Librarian's Guide to Personal Development: An Annotated Bibliography*. New York: Special Libraries Association, 1980.

Includes a small section on time management. Brief annotations for seven books and one cassette program. 24 pages.

Silcox, Diana, and Mary Ellen Moore. *Woman Time: Personal Time Management for Women Only*. New York: Wyden Books, 1980.

Based on interviews with women working outside of the home. Integrates techniques for managing time at home with those for work. Major topics include procrastination, delegation, interruptions, and dealing with family. 308 pages.

Thomas, P. A., and Valerie A. Ward. *Where the Time Goes*. London: Aslib, 1973.

Study of time spent by small group of British librarians at work. Results indicated that librarians spend much of their time on planned and unplanned meetings and work primarily in their offices. 43 pages.

Winston, Stephanie. *The Organized Executive: A Program for Productivity—New Ways to Manage Time, Paper, and People*. New York: Warner Books, 1983.

Part I contains detailed information on filing techniques and systems for handling paper records. Part II concerns time management. Use Master List and Daily Lists to manage tasks. Tips to reduce major time wasters: procrastination, meetings, and interruptions. Part III contains ideas for organizing staff. 345 pages.

Winwood, Richard I., and Hyrum W. Smith. *Excellence Through Time Management.* Salt Lake City, Utah: Franklin Institute, Inc., 1985.

> Time robbers can be externally imposed by the work environment or internally imposed. Productivity Pyramid illustrates the influences that values have on the planning process. Other major topics include strategies for meetings, procrastination, personal clutter, and interruptions. 138 pages.

ARTICLES

Ashkens, Ronald N., and Robert H. Schaffer. "Managers Can Avoid Wasting Time." *Harvard Business Review* 60 (May-June 1982): 98–104.

> Many time management techniques treat symptoms, ignore underlying problem—anxiety. Making demands of subordinates and improving performance under pressure, anxiety. Breaking tasks into smaller, well-defined projects to increase a sense of accountability and provide more predictable results of actions reduce anxiety.

Austin, Nancy K. "Race Against Time—and Win." *Working Woman* 15 (November 1990): 48–54.

> Six time wasters: unnecessary worrying, information overload, refusal to delegate control, failure to praise employees, misguided motivation, and too-strict adherence to rules.

Berner, Andrew. "The Importance of Time Management in the Small Library." *Special Libraries* 78 (Fall 1987): 271–76.

> Too many librarians hold myths about time management. Time management focuses on effectiveness (doing the right job) rather than efficiency (doing the job right). To learn the skills of time management, librarians must "unlearn" the myths.

Braid, Robert W. "Effective Use of Time." *Supervisory Management* 28 (July 1983): 9–14.

> Tips for dealing with procrastination, too much work, paperwork, and drop-in visitors.

Calano, Jimmy, and Jeff Salzman. "How to Get More Done in a Day." *Working Woman* 13 (April 1988): 99–100.

> Twelve tips involving planning, keeping good files, and reviewing work activities.

Callarman, William G., and William W. McCartney. "Reversing Reverse Delegation." *Management Solutions* 33 (July 1988): 11–15.

> How supervisors can avoid reverse delegation.

Collins, Helen Lippman. "When Your Job is Just One of Your Worries." *RN* 50 (August 1987): 60–62.

> To juggle work and other responsibilities, decide what are true priorities: forget unimportant things. Make lists and plan ahead to get everything accomplished.

Davidson, Jeffrey P. "Avoiding Interruptions: Time-Saving Plan Can Benefit You and Your Staff." *Data Management* 25 (August 1987): 17–18.

Reduce number of interruptions from staff members by training them to classify questions into four categories: 1) those addressed by policy manuals, 2) those that can be handled by coworkers, 3) those that can be handled by memo to manager or answered in two or three sentences, 4) those requiring face-to-face meeting with manager.

Douglass, Merrill E. "Do You Have to Suffer from All Those Interruptions?" *Management Solutions* 32 (July 1987): 40–43.

Telephone and drop-in interruption tips. Approach time management with problem-solving methods. Find specific problems, formulate solutions.

Douglass, Merrill E., and Donna N. Douglass. "Time Theft." *Personnel Administrator* 26 (September 1981): 13.

Time theft is largely a matter of attitude—taking longer lunch hours, socializing on work time, letting work expand to fit the time available.

Ferderber, Charles J. "10 Techniques for Managing Your Time More Effectively." *Practical Accountant* 14 (August 1981): 67–69.

Insulate yourself to capitalize on your controllable time. Concentrate on the most significant matters.

Fitzpatrick, Jean Grasso. "Time: Stop Working Late." *Working Woman* 8 (October 1983): 71–72.

Working late hours regularly indicates a problem. Workdays erode if workers take time before starting work with morning coffee and stretch lunch hours. Set goals and priorities on an hourly basis.

Gothberg, Helen M. "Time Management and the Woman Library Manager." *Library Journal* 112 (May 1, 1987): 37–40.

Tips for delegation, telephone interruptions, and meetings.

_____. "Time Management in Special Libraries." *Special Libraries* 82 (Spring 1991): 119–30.

Survey of special library directors indicates time management problems with meetings, telephone interruptions, drop-in visitors, inaccurate or delayed information, and estimating time unrealistically. Special library directors delegate more readily to staff members, but should train their staff members to delegate more.

Gothberg, Helen M., and Donald E. Riggs. "Time Management in Academic Libraries." *College and Research Libraries* 49 (March 1988): 131–40.

Librarians differ somewhat from other management groups in that they tend to estimate time unrealistically and take on too much at once. Personal disorganization contributes to poor time management. Time wasters include scheduled and unscheduled meetings and lack of clear communication.

Howland, Joan. "Effective Time Management: Work Smarter, Not Harder." *Trends in Law Library Management and Technology* 1 (April 1988): 2–6.

Establish goals and priorities, plan and schedule each day, avoid procrastination, and delegate effectively.

Kozumplik, William A. "Time and Motion Study of Library Operations." *Special Libraries* 58 (October 1967): 585–88.

Time and motion studies for library work can establish specific, realistic goals for performance. Staff morale improves from working toward well-defined goals and within specific performance standards.

Kurtz, Theodore. "10 Reasons Why People Procrastinate." *Supervisory Management* 35 (April 1990): 1–2.

Ten common reasons for procrastination. Few strategies offered for help.

Leach, Ronald G. "Finding Time You Never Knew You Had." *Journal of Academic Librarianship* 6 (March 1980): 4–8.

General time management advice: identify time wasters, identify important tasks and prioritize them. Brief information on delegation, procrastination, and uninterruptible time.

Mauro, Elsi H., and Weber, David C. "Time Management for Library Staff." *Journal of Library Administration* 1 (Winter 1980): 13–20.

General time management techniques, such as setting priorities, without specifically relating them to library work. Tips for handling stress and how management should become involved to solve time management problems.

Phillips, Steven R. "The New Time Management." *Training and Development Journal* 42 (April 1988): 73–77.

Values-based approach. Workers must be clear on which values matter more to them before they can set realistic and worthy goals. Includes time management, values clarification, and use of organizing notebook in staff training.

Raney, Carol. "Time Management in the Elementary School Media Center." *North Carolina Libraries* 46 (Spring 1988): 18–21.

Lists time management techniques according to the major functions for a media coordinator. Cultivating volunteer workers, building lines of communication with teachers, and using computers effectively.

Samuelson, Howard. "Increasing Public Library Productivity." *Library Journal* 106 (February 1, 1981): 309–11.

Work simplification (including some time management), work analysis, improved management, and employee motivation. Review statistics to eliminate those not needed.

Schwarz, Fred C. "Are You Managing Your Job?: or Is It Managing You?" *Wisconsin Library Bulletin* 75 (November 1979): 266–68.

Setting priorities and goals.

Stripling, Barbara. "Finding Time: Practical Time Management for Out-of-Classroom Educators." *Clearing House* 59 (January 1986): 225–27.

Setting personal goals and eliminating time wasters. Typical timewasters for librarians are expansion of routine tasks to fit time available, interruptions, and socializing.

Tucker, Raymond K. "Time Management." *Library Acquisitions: Practice & Theory* 13, no. 1 (1989): 37–38.

Communication techniques for avoiding interruptions.

AUDIOCASSETTES

How to Get Things Done. Shawnee Mission, Kans.: National Seminars, Inc., 1987.

Seminar program. Six cassettes and 18-page manual. Procrastination, meetings, and project planning.

Time Management. Overland Park, Kans.: Padgett-Thompson, 1987.

Seminar program. Six cassettes and 43-page manual. Priority planning, delegation, procrastination, interruptions, meetings.

Index

About the Author

J. WESLEY COCHRAN is the Law Library Director and Associate Professor of Law at Texas Tech University. His articles have appeared in several professional journals.

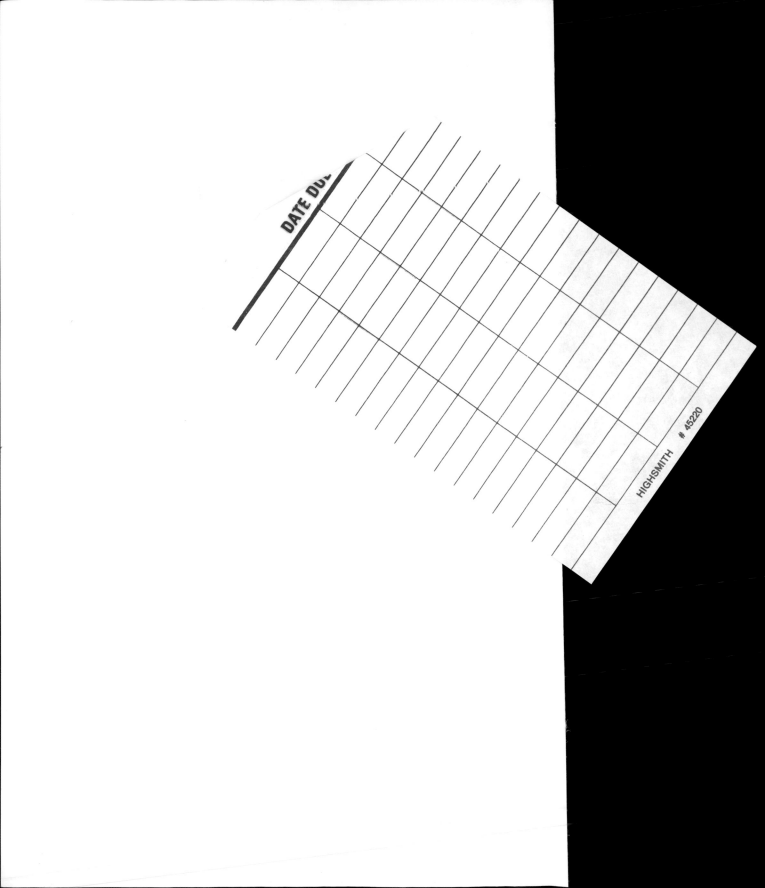

DATE DUE

HIGHSMITH   # 45220